# My Journey as a Belly Dancer

*Pix on front cover taken by a great friend, Fay Girling whilst we were in Malaga, Spain, with whom I spent many happy holidays over the years*

# MY JOURNEY AS A BELLY DANCER

Elizabeth Gordon

Matador
9 Priory Business Park,
Wistow Road, Kibworth Beauchamp,
Leicestershire. LE8 0RX
Tel: 0116 279 2299
Email: books@troubador.co.uk
Web: www.troubador.co.uk/matador
Twitter: @matadorbooks


ISBN 9781838594848

British Library Cataloguing in Publication Data.
A catalogue record for this book is available from the British Library.

Printed on FSC accredited paper
Printed and bound in Great Britain by 4edge Limited
Typeset in 11pt Minion Pro by Troubador Publishing Ltd, Leicester, UK

Matador is an imprint of Troubador Publishing Ltd

For
Hussein

"This is urgent," said my boss as I walked into the office from the dripping rain on a grey Monday morning. "I need it now," he kept repeating relentlessly as drops of water steadily fell from my umbrella, creating a wet pool around my feet.

I was a legal secretary working for solicitors in Holborn, London, and after arriving at the office at 9.30am on a Monday morning, I longed for the end of the week when I could leave at 5.30pm on a Friday evening, as the routine of the daily workload – typing one tape after another, day in and day out – felt more and more like an endurance test as the weeks and months went by.

I was only five minutes late but before I could remove my hat and coat, I was made to feel guilty that I was not already sitting at my desk, showing obedience and subservience to those I had to respect by busily typing and getting on with the work that had been left for me earlier that morning.

Time was of the essence in solicitors' offices as legal secretaries were under immense pressure to churn out as much work as they could in the hours allotted to them, and time wasters were unmentionably looked down upon and noticeably resented. The attitude was, 'if the kitchen is too hot, get out'. A lot did, but those who survived felt like conveyor belts to those in control, and the job was what I called 'a soul destroyer'!

I was thirty years of age, unmarried and looking for a hobby or an outlet to help the boredom I was experiencing. I felt locked to my desk with a ball and chain, frightened that the key was either lost or had been thrown away; a far cry from how it all started many years before.

★

My mother was an artist, having attained a scholarship as one of six students in the country for a place at Manchester School of Art, where her drawing of the nude back view of a young woman was admired enough to be hung above the stairs in the main college hall. L.S. Lowry quoted her as being "one of the coming artists of the day" in the Manchester Guardian after viewing one of her oil paintings, named 'Romiley Bridge', at a local exhibition in Cheshire.

At the age of twenty-three years, she wrote and illustrated a children's book called *The Adventures of Plonk*. As paints were rationed during the War, she was limited to using the only four colours available – red, green, yellow and black.

She started Plonk from drawing around a farthing, which formed part of its body, creating a Bambi/horse-like creature, black with yellow spots, wearing a bright red hat on his head that kept falling off in the wind and red boots on his feet.

The book was sold all over the world after being published in 1944, a year before the end of the War, by Franklyn Ward & Wheeler Ltd, based in Leicester; and hundreds of copies were piled high in the shape of a pyramid at Lewis's, a large store in Manchester where my mother spent hours signing copies for the public.

She was an only child, a vivacious, bubbly lady, warm and artistic, highly sensitive with a temperamental nature, but was always looked upon as a bit of a rebel within her strict family group, as all her uncles were practising Methodist Ministers and her grandfather was Principal of Hartley College who taught young men to be theologians. My mother often shocked them by coming home with pictures of nudes she had drawn that day at the Art College, which were very often not looked upon in the best of grace.

In 1945 she met Louis whilst he was staying at her friends Lottie and Johnny's house. They were helping to rehabilitate him back into civil life after he was demobbed from serving in the British Army at the end of the War.

At the age of 16 years he ran away from his Russian Jewish background to join the British Army and was sent to Israel with his regiment during the 1936-1939 Palestine conflict. Whilst there, he learnt Christ's teachings which changed his life whereupon he was baptised in the River Jordan to become Christian. Then WW2 broke out enforcing him to spend 9 years in the Army, which was much longer than he originally intended.

He was tall, handsome and charismatic, and my mother was swept off her feet the moment she met him and they married in 1946. I was born three years later in Maidenhead, Berkshire, and my brother Jeremy was born two years after me in Leamington Spa, Warwickshire.

After leaving the Army, my father taught English and English Literature in schools and colleges around the country, not settling anywhere in particular until I was five, when my parents bought a plot of land in Seaford, East Sussex. This was easily available to purchase at the end of the war as parts of the town had been noticeably bombed, reducing some of the buildings to rubble, after the Germans had emptied their cargo along the south coast before returning to their homeland.

My mother created the plans to build a house there by the sea called 'Schooners', down College Road, with a beautiful bay window at the front. The garden at the back of the house was made up of pebbles, all different sizes and shapes, collected from the beach; and in the summer, masses of marigolds that were intermingled between the stones blossomed in full colour, inspiring my mother to paint them in all their brilliance, a splendid orange spectacle of oils on canvas.

During the Queen's Coronation in 1953, the country arranged facilities for the public to watch the enthronement of the Queen live on television, and Seaford was no exception. Three black and white television sets were placed on the stage in a school hall so that a packed audience could witness the event. Being a special occasion, the kindergarten I attended nearby presented all the children at the nursery with a Queen Elizabeth II coronation mug, which contained two packets of Spangles that I was eager to open but my mother would not allow me to eat them until after dinner, which was a great sacrifice as I much preferred the thought of eating the sweets than having to eat dinner.

My father was fortunate enough to own a portable typewriter during the War. He wrote shows to entertain the troops and created jokes for a two-man gag show in which he played the straight man. One of the jokes went: "Were you brought up at Eton?" "No, I was eaten and brought up!" and another: "We are all here to help others, but what the others are here for, God knows!"

In my parents' spare time, they made puppets from paper mache, painting and clothing them to represent different characters from well-known nursery rhymes and children's storybooks. They practised enhancing their voices to synchronise with the character of the puppet until it sounded professional, and when they became confident enough in their technique they called themselves "The Gordon Puppets" and toured the south east of England exhibiting shows for young children. When I peeped through the drawn curtains on the stage, I sensed an atmosphere of anticipation and excitement that the theatre is known to capture and with the school halls filled with young families eagerly waiting to see the show, I loved watching the children's enchantment and laughter as the puppets took on a life of their own.

After four years of teaching my father accepted that the profession never truly suited his heart and, needing something more invigorating to occupy him, he rented out offices in Brighton to start a career in business, and became involved in the property market.

Over the years he became a successful businessman and eventually became Company Director of a group of companies named MIAS, occupying Peter Seller's old offices in Park Lane, London, overlooking Hyde Park – which enabled us to have a wonderful lifestyle.

As my father's company rapidly grew, my parents left Seaford, moving many times until we settled in a house called 'Windmill Down' in Neville Road, Rottingdean, high on the cliff and overlooking the coastline towards Brighton. It was in a superb location, next to the golf course and adjacent to the South Downs, with its stylish yellow French shutters and grand entrance.

Even though we were laid back from the main road, because of our position on the cliff facing the sea, there were times when strong gusts of wind would playfully swirl around the house – and especially at night, eerie tones like bugle noises trumpeted through the windows, disturbing us from our sleep until we learnt how to accept those mischievous sounds as part of the uniqueness of living there.

In the back garden there was a tiny summer house which Jeremy and I decorated with old bits of carpet that we laid on the floorboards, cushions on empty paint tins turned upside down that we could sit on, and a large cardboard box that we used as a table where we played all our games – Monopoly, Draughts and cards – out of sight from our parents.

Nestled amongst the South Downs, at the back of our garden stood a smock windmill, erected in 1802 by Thomas Beard in all its glory as a landmark for many miles around. Our little black dachshund, Sammy, would race my brother and I to the windmill and back, wearing his bright red woolly coat – knitted by my mother to keep him warm in the cold winter months – which enabled us to spot him when he jumped over the tufts of grass, trying to keep up with us as we ran across the Downs.

Having moved so many times in my earlier years and having already attended a number of schools by the time I was eight, as there were no places available at Roedean nearby, my parents suggested that I go to boarding school for stability and enticed me to choose one from a list in the Guide Book of Schools. As Lavant House School for Girls in Chichester was also an equestrian school where I could learn to ride, I persuaded my parents to agree with my choice.

My full name was printed on white satin tags that had to be attached to all of my belongings, and my mother and I spent hours sewing them onto my school uniform, sheets, pillowcases, nightwear, riding attire – including the hat and boots, sports clothes, outdoor and indoor shoes, and leisure weekend clothes. My name was also placed on bathroom items so that they would not be lost or misused.

I learnt from a very young age the mixture of emotions connected with the upheaval of leaving one's home and family, even though I had been given a certain amount of freedom in choosing the school of my choice!

All my belongings went into a gigantic trunk with my name printed on the front in big black letters, which was picked up by a courier and forwarded onto the school before my arrival. Then later that same day, my father drove us by car along the coast from Rottingdean to Chichester, where we all stayed in a hotel in the town centre overnight.

In the morning after breakfast, I put my new school uniform on – a pastel mint green blazer with grey skirt and a smart green velour hat to finish – and my mother came into the hotel bedroom with my little brother to say their goodbyes away from public view. Jeremy wrapped his arms around me. I could see us both in the dressing table mirror and recognising that I was going to miss him more than I realised, I squeezed him to remind him to remember me whilst I was gone. I then said my sad goodbyes to my mother, who was trying to fight back the tears, and my father took me downstairs to the main foyer of the hotel to collect his car and drive me to the school.

On the short journey, my father was in a sombre mood. We did not talk much to one another, but I felt he was sensitive to my feelings and wanted me to know that he did love me very much. I was not sure what to expect but having been to a number of schools in my earlier life, including kindergartens, I felt I had already gained some experience of the challenges of what could lie ahead, although I had not fully realised how different life might be by not returning home at the end of the day.

We arrived at the driveway of the school and the headmistress, Mrs Green, an elderly lady with white hair wearing a plaid tweed skirt, lisle stockings and flat shoes, was waiting for us with a simple smile as we went through the security gates to approach her at the main entrance of the school. She explained that my belongings had already arrived and were waiting for me in one of the dormitories upstairs, which she would show me later, and then there was an ominous silence. I was being passed over. My father leant down to hug me before he left and said he hoped I would be happy there. I watched his back view disappear into the distance, tall and distinguished, as he got into his car to return to the hotel in Chichester town centre where my mother and brother were waiting for his return.

*

For the first night or two at boarding school I suffered terrible homesickness, but I learnt how to survive and took solace with the horses, learning how to ride. I found the trot very difficult to master at first, until I rode bareback on Lucky, a lovely old bay, riding him back to the stables each day after he had been grazing in the field nearby. The next time I got on a horse saddled up, I found that the experience of trotting was a far more pleasurable one than it had been at first.

I was one of six girls in the dormitory and Beverley, of my same age group, was asked to show me around and how to fit in with the school routine. She was a bit of a tomboy with long blonde hair and blue eyes, and when Matron put the lights out at night after prayers, she would come over to my bed and whisper to me, talking about anything and everything that came into her head. Her Father was Alan Weeks, the well-known BBC swimming and sports commentator, and she had an elder sister also boarding at the school, who spent most of her time in the stables looking after the horses. Even though Beverley was a weekly boarder returning home at the weekends, she was lonely, needed a friend, and so did I.

I missed her company dreadfully when her parents came to collect her on Saturday mornings, not only because I was left with boarders much older than myself to communicate with at the weekends but because I was a three-weekly boarder and only able to see my parents every third Sunday. On those occasions, we were limited to just a couple of hours, giving us just enough time to return to the hotel where they were staying in Chichester for tea and cakes, before returning to school later that evening which was always a wrench when we had to part.

One of the girls in my dormitory, Suzy, was not happy with Beverley coming over to whisper to me after lights out and she told her elder sister Mary that our chatting was keeping her awake, which caused some controversy, and out of the blue, Suzy told me that her sister Mary wanted to have a fight with me.

When I told Beverley what had happened, she said she

would show me some moves to protect myself and the next night, knowing everyone in the dormitory was asleep, she crept over to my bed, telling me to be quiet, and pinned me down with her legs and knees, asking me to see if I could free myself from her grip. I tried with all my might to escape from her grasp, but it proved impossible, and she taught me how to defend myself against all adversary.

The day arrived for the fight and all the girls from Mary's class were encircled outside in the grounds after school hours, besides everyone from my class, waiting for the spectacle to begin.

I was eight years old, the new girl and the underdog. Mary was eleven, tall and popular. The girls were waiting. I entered the circle, focusing on Mary, who was waiting for me, ready, knowing everyone was on her side. I was shorter than she in stature and after a bit of arm grabbing, clothes pulling and unnecessary clinging, I managed to free myself from her clutches by deliberately crouching down and getting hold of both her legs to make her fall to the ground. Then I pinned her down, like Beverley had shown me, making sure she could not budge from her position. The girls were yelling around us.

The fight was short and sweet as the next thing I was aware of, was a firm grip on my shoulder. It was Matron, telling us to stop what we were doing and to get up at once. I released my hold and we both stood up, looking hot and flustered.

"What is going on?" said Matron. We had no answer, but I was relieved the ordeal was over and as I looked up at the sad expression on Mary's face, noticing that she was about to cry and understanding that Matron wanted us to make it up, I put my arm around her in the hope that we could be friends. A slow smile gradually emerged on her lips that cut across the tears lying on her rosy plump cheeks, and as she reciprocated by wrapping her arm around my waist, I felt a sense of comfort, realising that she also wanted to make it up and be friends. We had not met properly before; we only knew about each other through her sister Suzy. When Matron realised everything was going to be alright, she accepted we had learnt from the experience without needing further punishment.

After Matron left the scene, some of the girls came over and clapped me on my back, saying 'well done'. It felt strange that although a few weeks earlier, no one had taken much notice of my arrival or shared much interest in knowing who I was, suddenly to become popular, especially amongst the younger day girls, within a very short space of time. I was even treated to a midnight feast by Beverley and the other boarders who had collected sweets and cakes over the weeks for such an event as a form of celebration; and Beverley's elder sister, who spent a lot of time in the stables, made sure I got a leg up on the horses, which was an honour against those who had to struggle to get on the horse by themselves.

After that event I began to settle at the school and on a Saturday Matron would organise groups of us to visit Chichester town centre to buy sweets and other things we might need from our pocket money. On Sundays, after visiting the local church in Lavant for the morning service, we would get together for long walks across the country on trails prepared earlier by one of the girls in the sixth form, and we generally returned back to school with muddy boots, which we had to clean and polish ourselves before tea. Besides the organised events arranged by Matron and some of the older boarders, there was always the chance to ride the horses or help in the stables, in our spare time if we chose to.

One Sunday, the boarders were asked to create a character from a classical children's book from old clothes that had been collected over the years and kept in a large trunk for that purpose. There was a competition as to who could characterise the best act on the stage and it was to be performed in front of the headmistress and the rest of the school staff. By the time I had a chance to look through the garments in the trunk there was hardly anything left apart from two old football or rugby shirts when an idea came into my mind. I then needed to find two schoolboys' caps, which I was lucky enough to spot at the bottom of the trunk as I hoped to characterise Tweedledum and Tweedledee as they were portrayed by Lewis Carroll in the classic fictional book of 'Alice in Wonderland' where portly twin boys grinned the whole time they recited poetry. I had to find a partner and managed to persuade a girl of my same height to join me. As Tweedledum and Tweedledee were plump in stature, we put extra clothing underneath our shirts to create more of a likeness to their shape. The performance was not to take too long on the stage, so we only learnt a couple of verses of the poem they sang from the book and worked on a little jig to go with it. The difficult part of the act was to keep grinning throughout the performance without looking unnatural! On the day of the competition I thought the other contestants were brilliant and felt that whatever the result, there had been a lot of fun in organising it. When the announcement of the winner or winners was declared I was dumbfounded to hear that we had won! We both felt marvellous collecting our prize from Mrs Green, the headmistress, which was a box full of different flavoured lollipops. Not wanting to look greedy, we decided to share our prize with the other boarders who openly appreciated our generosity.

★

During the summer breaks from boarding school, I was fortunate enough to enjoy some wonderful holidays with my parents, travelling through Europe and visiting Nice, and staying in Monte Carlo, Madrid and the lovely little town of Alassio, near Genoa. But when visiting Barcelona I saw my first bull fight, which horrified me and was something I never wanted to see again.

We also visited Tangier in north Africa, staying in a five-star hotel, El Minzah, with its Arabesque woodwork, arched doorways and oriental carpets overlooking stunning views of the bay of Tangier. My father organised a guide to show us around Morocco, where we toured the markets, rode camels on the edge of the Sahara desert and spent a memorable evening in a kasbah, which was a private affair other than sharing with an American family who sat opposite us to witness Arabic musicians play glorious music as we dined till late into the evening. Jeremy and I were allowed to stay up that night as a special occasion, and later on a beautiful adolescent boy, bare-chested but wearing a fez and pantaloon trousers that were kept up by coloured scarves embedded with coins around his hips, danced sensuously to the music in front of us. I was immediately captivated and believe I experienced the first pangs of love.

When he left the stage, the musicians carried on playing and my father asked me to get up and dance to the music. I was far too shy. He begged me and the musicians were waiting, but sadly I had to let everyone down as I could not get myself up onto the black and white squared dance floor, disappointing my father greatly.

★

When I was ten and a half, reaching eleven, I heard the news that my mother was going through a rough patch in her marriage with my father and she wanted me to return home to live with her in Rottingdean, which meant leaving all my friends behind at Lavant House without much notice. Living at home was not easy to adapt to at first as I already felt I had been given my independence from the young age of eight in having to survive my own battles and rectify my own problems, and I found it difficult to accept that I was not only under a parent's control once again but also had to play the part of protector towards my mother, who was needing my emotional support.

In the meantime, I attended St Martha's Convent as a day girl – which was close to home in the heart of the village of Rottingdean, near The Plough Inn and the duck pond, and where Rudyard Kipling once lived. The Convent School accepted me as a Church of England Protestant, and to my bewilderment selected me from my class to perform as one of four girls in a dance group at the school bazaar. I had no idea why they had chosen me as I had not particularly shown dancing qualities, but I took up the challenge nonetheless. We were shown our paces, which we were instructed to practise, and for months before the actual day of the performance I drove my parents to distraction going around the house murmuring, "Step together, hop, point, step together, hop, point," which I practised at every available moment until the day arrived when I was supposed to show off what I could do.

The bazaar was to be held outside in the grounds of the school and on my arrival, I was surprised to learn that we were to wear a national Welsh costume for the dancing event, which we had not prepared for. When I tried it on the whole regalia felt very uncomfortable, particularly the tall pointed hat, which I found difficult to balance on top of my head, and as we had not had any rehearsals to accustom ourselves to the outfit before the show, I wondered how I was going to move in it, never mind dance in it!

Later that afternoon when everybody began to arrive, I hoped my parents would be amongst the audience. They had promised they would attend to see how well I could perform as their expectations were high, especially after having put up with my practising the steps around them for so long.

When the music started I led the group onto the stage, and being at the end of the row I immediately found I was in difficulty synchronising with the other girls due to the strangeness of wearing the cumbersome costume whilst at the same time having to balance the hat on my head, which I felt could drop off at any moment. The music seemed to be ahead of me, and I soon found I was having trouble focusing and concentrating on the steps when I thought I could spot my parents and little brother in the distance amongst the crowds laughing and in fits of giggles. I could not understand what had caused their laughter until I joined them afterwards, when my mother said, "Well, you will never be a dancer, darling," and I realised I must have done something wrong. They described how my feet were pointing upwards, unlike the others and that when I was dancing to the left, everyone else was edging towards the right, besides my arms rotating all over the place. It was obviously a complete catastrophe, but as I had no intention of looking at dancing as a career, I was able to shrug the matter off quite well, especially after my parents reassured me that I looked wonderful in my new costume and it was not the end of the world. In any case, I was more gratified that they had made the effort to show their presence under the circumstances, as I knew they were both going through difficulties with one another, and putting all our troubles aside, we were able to enjoy the rest of the afternoon by joining in with the organised activities.

There was the tombola, various raffles and spinning the wheel, where my father was lucky enough to win a bottle of whisky, which pleased him no end. Amazingly, Jeremy won the horticultural show with his simple collection of a few wild flowers that he had picked from the Downs earlier that morning which he had placed in a plain glass of water minutes before, much to the annoyance of all the other contributors who had spent hours preparing their arrangements. By the end of the day, I had forgotten all about 'step together, hop, point' and the fact that I had shown difficulty with coordination of movement, as it was something I did not really feel I needed to worry about.

★

By the time I was thirteen my parents had divorced, and my mother, brother and I moved to a roomy flat in Brighton overlooking New Steine. It meant further upheaval in getting used to a new environment, making new friends and changing schools once again, but I was fortunate enough to be accepted by The Blessed Sacrament Convent School in Brighton as a Church of England Protestant. It was within walking distance from home and Reverend Mother introduced me to Julia, the only other Protestant at the school who happened to be in my class. She was a tall, athletic girl, having swum for the Junior Championship of Sussex, lithesome with blonde hair and blue eyes.

As Julia and I were not expected to study the teachings of Catechism or join the other pupils for daily prayers at the school, we played tennis together within the school grounds, enabling us to get to know each other and become good friends. Later on, I learnt that her younger brother, Rupert, was in the same class as Jeremy at Brighton College, which we found to be an extraordinary coincidence and occasionally arranged foursomes at the weekends.

★

My parents remained friends even though they both lived their separate lives after their divorce and my father always stayed in contact with me and my brother as we were growing up, taking us out on trips in the car along the south coast, meals out and visits to the cinema, which we both enjoyed as he kept us amused being an entertaining, worldly, interesting man.

My mother got more involved in her artwork and she met D'Oyly John, a well-known artist who lived in Rottingdean, surviving his talent by earning a good living from selling his pictures in a shop down Preston Street in Brighton. An interesting character, he told us that he was second cousin to Augustus John and admitted that when he was wounded by a bomb in 1945, which temporarily blinded him, the incident added to his artistic abilities in the way of how he viewed colour. He was well known to paint scenes mainly of the French and Spanish Riviera and his style inspired my mother to paint oils with a palette knife, creating some wonderful pictures of her own.

Besides my mother's artwork, she took an interest in the Spiritualist movement, whose teachings she felt an affinity with, and at the age of fourteen I was able to join and attend the services with her. We went to a little place down St James's Street called Brotherhood Gate Church, which was concealed down the side of an alleyway, past a bakery. We tried to disguise where we were going as the Spiritualist movement had mixed views with the outside public, so we took a quick turn to the right into the alleyway, hoping no one would see us. Nevertheless, I became impressed with the meetings and lectures on the philosophy of the movement, besides some of the demonstrations given by mediums. A Spiritual artist painted some of my previous lives: China, Tibet and my last life, Egypt. There was nothing to prove that she was correct, but I was fascinated with her analogy whether it was true or not and accepted it for what it was worth.

Around that same age I had an out-of-body experience, where I felt myself rising from my body with a floating sensation until I thought I could touch the ceiling and saw my body on the bed.

Intrigued, I wanted to travel further, to leave the safety of the bedroom, and found myself being pulled along through a dark tunnel similar to an umbilical cord as I approached joyous crowds both sides of me, smiling and waving, with people from the Middle East acting as though they knew me, greeting me and cheering me on. I was not fully understanding their affection towards me but I was enjoying their attention and did not want it to end. Eventually, I came to a point where I felt a powerful force blocking my way. I accepted that it was my guide, who I believed to be Chinese, barring me from going further without thought. I wanted to carry on and insisted he let me pass but sensed the integrity of his wisdom in asking me to reflect on my better judgment by returning to finish the journey that had been planned for me. I knew I had reached the crossroads and that it was time to make a decision, and having understood his message, which was transferred to me telepathically, I reluctantly but obediently turned around to face the daunting process of reuniting with my body.

On my descent I felt lost and a sense of panic began to set in as I realised how far I had travelled. Then at that moment a wave of calm overwhelmed me, enabling me to move speedily through the darkness of the tunnel. I felt I was gravitating backwards into a density, unlike my experience earlier, and hoped I would see the crowds again to uplift me and cheer me on my way, but when I approached them again, their faces were looking downwards, away from me, solemn and glum, and wondered why when they were so rapturous earlier. Then, quite vividly, I saw a man dressed in dark garments standing by a car, smiling, and even though I could not recognise him, I sensed I knew him somehow.

Soon after, without warning, I suddenly found myself on the ceiling in my bedroom and I was horrified to see my body on the bed, believing it was impossible to reunite, and panic started to set in again. A moment or two later, that same powerful force of calm surrounded me as I found myself lying horizontally just a couple of inches above my body. Once again, panic set in for a moment or two before a shroud of calmness, like a veil of tranquillity, overtook the fear as the adjustment and synchronisation took place. Relieved, feeling I was reunited with my body, the first thing I did was check to see if I could move my fingers. Yes, I was fine. Then gradually, as the feelings grew from my fingers to my hands, I felt a strangeness, as though I had foreign arms with an abundance of bangles all around them, and I was gesticulating movements unfamiliar to me. It faded after a while but the whole experience had left its powerful impression upon me and I drew an outline of the face of the gentleman who I had seen on my journey the next morning.

*

In my mid-teens I was eager to show society I belonged to a group of people I felt akin to and I dressed as a Mod, wearing suede or leather jackets, mini-skirts and white ankle boots, with my hair shaped long at the front and short at the back – a Vidal Sassoon cut – like many other girls who wanted the same style. The male Mods were smart, wearing polo-neck sweaters and tailored suits with slim-fitting pants, and their hair was a mop-top style resembling an ordinary kitchen mop, which was a mid-length hairstyle, collar-length at the back and over the ears at the sides with a straight fringe, named after and popularised by The Beatles.

A lot of them owned scooters, either a Lambretta or a Vespa, and wore military parkas to keep their clothes clean whilst riding. They spent time in chosen coffee shops that had an indoor jukebox. Their lives centred around listening to the latest pop songs in tiny booths at record shops without the obligation of having to buy, and in the evening on a Saturday night they attended dances at the Sussex universities, where they could enjoy the music played by live bands.

In Brighton, on my first visit to the Hippodrome, I was lucky enough to get tickets for the front row where I saw pop groups such as Jerry and the Pacemakers, Dave Berry, Herman Hermits, the omnipotent Roy Orbison and of course, my favourites, The Beatles, play live on stage. The atmosphere was unbelievable, with a lot of high-pitched screaming from the teenagers making it difficult to hear the music as the groups' amplifiers were not powerful enough to be heard above the intense noise of the fans' excited enthusiasm. When the curtains gradually rose, I tried to hold my excitement in check by managing not to scream when The Beatles appeared live on the stage, as I wanted to save my energy to remember every second of their performance. It was the beginning of Beatlemania and I was swept up in the euphoria of it all, and after the show I eagerly joined crowds of other fans at the back of the theatre to watch the Fabulous Four wave and smile at us through the window of their dressing room. It was a magical moment. My favourite was George.

After that experience I bought tickets to see many bands in Brighton including The Searches, Moody Blues, The Hollies, Freddy and the Dreamers and Dusty Springfield, to name but a few.

In 1964 I witnessed the Mod and Rocker fights in Brighton from the safety of our home overlooking New Steine, and watched swarms of young men and women ransacking everything in sight. It was terrifying to watch. Eventually they swelled onto Brighton beach, where the police battled with them and managed to arrest a fair number of the troublemakers and ringleaders.

It was a teenage post-war revolution of liberalisation, a strange exhilarating feeling of freedom against authority and suppression. The 1960s teenagers were changing the face of Britain, sweeping through the country, and it was an opportunity to show an expression of identity en masse, the new generation being talented, fashionable and free. No one was going to stop them.

★

When Julia and I left school in our late teens, we decided to undertake a walk along the south coast from Brighton to Seaford, approximately eleven miles, hoping to stay the night and return by foot the next day, completely unaware that we might need practice or preparation for such a challenge.

We met outside the Undercliff Walk from Black Rock in Brighton and naively set off on our journey along the promenade overlooking the sea. The tide was out enough to see the remnants of the unique railway line nicknamed Daddy Long-Legs in Rottingdean – as it was usually covered by the sea but built to travel through the shallow waters of the coastline during 1896 to 1901, being a very popular service of that era – and we saw groups of children collecting fossils in buckets under the supervision of a parent or teacher, taking advantage of the ebbing tide.

On our way we sang songs and recited all the pop bands we knew, happily talking about anything that came into our minds as we approached the cliff edge of Saltdean to pause for a moment and reflect on the beautiful scenic views around us. Then we made our way along the grass verge towards Telscombe Cliffs to stop for a while at the Wimpy Bar on top of the hill, overlooking the sea, where we watched the yachts in full sail in the distance enjoying the calm seas as the sun glistened on the ocean in places, like tiny fairy lights scattered around, sparkling amidst the tiny waves.

Feeling more refreshed after having had something to eat, we eventually left the beautiful views of the coastline to walk inland through the never-ending, meandering pavements of Peacehaven, passing rows upon rows of individual bungalows with well-kept gardens showing off similar flowers, where the wind or neighbours had obviously shared seeds and cuttings with one another.

There was no nucleus point of a town centre or planned high street in Peacehaven, with small plots of land having been bought by separate owners just after the war – similar to Seaford, with just one or two local shops dotted amongst the houses. As we further strolled along the roadside, we eventually arrived at Newhaven, where we decided to sit on a wooden bench and watch the ferries depart from the harbour on their long four-hour voyage to Dieppe at the mouth of the River Ouse.

Whilst observing the activities of the harbour, where heavy freight was being offloaded from the ships, we felt a certain sense of excitement and adventure as we watched the movement of passengers, still in their cars, boarding the ferries. We let time slip by, when suddenly we noticed small patches of clouds accumulating amongst the ever-changing colours of the horizon and without further warning, we took heed and left before the weather could quickly play tricks on us.

With still a fair way to go, we sauntered through the residential parts of Newhaven along the main road, passing shops and houses, and as the skies began to threaten nightfall, we suddenly saw a few lights twinkling in the distance, recognising them to be our sleepy seaside town destination. But the feeling of triumph did not last long as we still had a fair distance to go and found ourselves wading through the tufts of grass along the roadside, which lay in droves, wild and coarse from the sea air. Not being able to sit or stop anywhere, with exhaustion and weariness setting in, we were beginning to wonder whether we should have remained in Peacehaven for our overnight stay.

It was not until we passed an old sign – 'Welcome to Seaford' – hidden amongst the foliage that we realised we had finally arrived. It was a bit of an anti-climax as there was no fanfare to greet us or anyone around to congratulate us, all we saw was an old man taking his dog out for a walk before settling in for the night, but we carried on regardless, trudging past closed shops and shut-up premises along the high street in the hope that we would eventually find somewhere to stay.

Our hopes began to diminish as the evening wore on and in our dilemma, we decided to wander down towards the esplanade to see what we could find along the seafront, when a wind started to pick up and we could hear the waves in the distance deepen in their intensity as they crashed against the stones on the shoreline, with the surge of the pebbles pulling back into the sea after the force of the wave had landed. There was a nip in the air and we sensed the gravity of the need to find somewhere to stay before it was too late. I saw my old house, 'Schooners', in the distance with the lights shining from the windows, looking cosy and warm, and I wondered if the new occupiers would take pity on us and let us have a room for the night.

Just as desperation started to set in, to our delight we saw a notice displayed in a window porch saying 'B&B Vacancies Available'. We could not believe our luck and pressed the tiny bell on the side wall in the hope that someone would answer. The door gradually opened and a cheery lady with curly blonde hair greeted us with a big smile, saying she was more than happy to take us in as there were two spare single rooms available upstairs, overlooking the sea, that needed occupancy. She kindly made us ham and cheese sandwiches, which we took to our rooms, and after a lovely hot bath I clambered into bed and slept soundly for the rest of the night.

The next morning, we were awoken by the gulls flying close overhead and looked forward to a hearty English breakfast to help us on our journey before venturing back home. It was only when we tried to climb down the stairs towards the dining room that we noticed our bodies ached more than we had first realised and, believing it to be a temporary problem that could be cured after breakfast, the landlady joined in with the spirited chatter of our sincere intentions of walking all the way back to Brighton, giving us the support we needed.

As we left the B&B, she wished us well and waved to us through the window as we set off in good cheer towards Newhaven, but it did not take long before we needed to rest. We found a spot on the grass verge along the roadside in the hope that we could find some extra impetus and energy to finish off our challenge. It was a beautiful fresh morning. with the sun shining and not a cloud in the sky. We overheard the familiar sounds of the gulls squawking in the distance as we watched them play over the waves of the sea and fascinated by their habits we found ourselves lulled into a sense of drowsiness that forced us to lay our heads on the tufts of grass, where we both dropped off to sleep in exhaustion.

Two hours later, we could not believe we had slept so soundly in such an open area without being disturbed by anyone and reluctantly rose from our cosy patch in the hope that we could muster some energy to finish our journey. To our disappointment, we knew we could not carry on any further and whether we liked it or not, we had to accept that it was time to acknowledge defeat. We did not want to, but there was nothing else for us to consider other than doing the sensible thing – by catching the bus to get ourselves back home.

★

Employment was scarce for young women in the early 1960s, with little choice other than working as cleaners, shop assistants or secretaries. As I had just finished my first year at the Secretarial College in Brighton, with RSA II in both typing and shorthand, at the age of sixteen I accepted the first job that was offered to me at Whitehead and Whitehead, estate agents in The Lanes, Brighton, as a typist.

I was on the top floor of a very tall building, sitting in a room with ten elderly gentlemen in their late fifties, sixties and even seventies, who were simultaneously tapping away for most of the day on their adding machines. Tap, tap, tap, brrrrr, brrrrr, brrrrr, as a reel of paper rolled out of the other end with figures neatly printed and automatically calculated. Their work consisted of adding up price lists of licensed stock for the pubs, clubs and liquor premises that they frequently visited during their business hours in Brighton and south-eastern areas; my job was to type out the stock schedules for all the wines, spirits and beers bought from all over the world, on an old Underwood manual typewriter.

They were a friendly crowd, cracking the odd joke now and again to pass the time, and even though I was the only female and youngster amongst them, I enjoyed their company. One factor I could not get used to was the heavy mixture of pipe and cigarette smoke that encircled the room all day, making it such a relief to get out at lunch time and feel the wind brush through my hair as I walked along the promenade towards the pier, breathing in the glorious, fresh salty sea air of the Brighton coastline.

The best part of the job was getting paid at the end of the week and every Friday afternoon, the staff would collect their wages from the accounts office. I received four £1 notes, a ten-shilling note, and four shillings and six pence in coins, neatly sealed in a manila envelope. With the first pay packet of my working life, I bought my mother some flowers to celebrate.

After I had been there a couple of months, a young man called Rob joined the group, eager to learn the trade; a handsome young man with strong, steely blue eyes and rugged features, bearing a confidence about him that was impressive for his eighteen years. They placed him on a large table opposite me and sometimes during the day I could sense his eyes focusing in my direction, as though he was weighing me up, and I felt uncomfortable as I knew I was not attracted to him.

My lack of interest, though, did not seem to stop him from having the courage to ask me out, which I thought was either brave or crazy on his part, considering that he must have sensed my disinterest with his earlier advances – but being curious and needing the experience of a first date, I accepted his offer.

We went to the cinema to see *Bullitt*, starring Steve McQueen, where we sat on the back row. Throughout the film, I could feel he was trying to edge towards me, which was nerve-racking as I waited for the inevitable. Eventually, I turned to face him and he kissed me, thrusting his lips into mine. It was what I believed to be my first real kiss. All my friends had been kissed on the back row at the cinema and I felt it was time to experience what they had on their first dates, accepting it was something one had to go through at that age. I did not know if I liked it or not, or that I enjoyed it, little realising in my naivety that one had to have feelings for the other person to get much out of it!

Returning to the office, I felt embarrassed, wondering if all the old gentlemen sensed what had happened between us. Even though I did not go out with him again, about a month or two afterwards, to my utter surprise, he asked me to marry him. I was thoroughly taken aback as I did not know him well enough to make such an important decision and marriage had not entered my head – with him or anyone – at the time, and I felt very uncomfortable having to refuse his offer as I genuinely did not want to hurt him. But it was my first lesson in understanding what difficulties could occur when going out with someone from the workplace, unless that person was very special.

Quite a few years later, when I was travelling home on a bus from Brighton Station that got stuck in the traffic at the Clock Tower, I happened to see Rob walking in the street with his arm around a lady who was pushing a baby in a pram, and they both stopped to look in a shop selling furniture. In a strange way, I wondered if I had let go of an opportunity that had come my way, yet at the same time I sensed that I had done the right thing and was relieved that I was not that lady. It was obviously something he wanted early in his life – a family and a home – which I knew I could not give him and I was genuinely pleased that he had finally found what he was looking for.

★

Over the six months that I had been working in the firm I boasted to my friends about how I knew the names of obscure wines, spirits and beers that none of them had ever heard of before. My mother also enjoyed learning about the existence of Chinese, Italian and South African wines, along with other exotic alcoholic drinks unfamiliar to her when she soon realised that I was not using my shorthand skills and became concerned that I would lose them if I did not get any proper secretarial practice. So, she got in touch with a friend of hers, Tom Sargent OBE (the founder of 'Justice'), who was in the middle of changing secretaries, and asked him if he would kindly give me the opportunity of working in his London offices to gain some valuable experience to further my career.

As Tom's new secretary was not to start for a couple of months, he accepted my offer of helping him before her arrival and at the age of sixteen, reaching seventeen, I made the daily commute by catching the 7.55am train from Brighton to Victoria, arriving in London at 8.55am. There I queued to catch the No.11 bus, a well-known route that passed some of the most renowned landmarks in London: Westminster Abbey, the Houses of Parliament, Whitehall, Trafalgar Square and, before Fleet Street, the iconic Royal Courts of Justice.

Bowler-hatted men filled the streets wearing pinstriped

suits, carrying rolled-up umbrellas, openly advertising their interest in the stocks and shares by proudly clutching the Financial Times close to their chests. Everyone appeared noticeably courteous and considerate, generally looking out for one another, airing a sense of purpose that differed from that of the tourists and holidaymakers I was used to in Brighton. It was also generally the case that whilst travelling on the bus or the tube, if passengers were not deliberately hiding behind their newspapers, I was offered a seat - just because I was a woman.

Tom's office was cut off from Fleet Street, down an alleyway, Crane Court. It was sparse with a tiny kitchen. He was aristocratic, tall, bearing a stoop, with dark brown penetrating eyes. A mop of white hair frequently fell over his thick black eyebrows as he spoke with an extraordinarily deep voice. I found him to be of a serious nature and always felt he had little humour, but that might have been because of my age.

He greeted me warmly on my arrival, showing me where the kitchen was to make a cup of tea or coffee and where I was to sit. At first, he gave me short letters to take down in shorthand, mixing the workload with some letters he had written in longhand, hoping I could decipher his writing and accustom myself with some of the legal jargon if I was going to progress as a legal secretary.

A lot of well-known barristers and QCs came into the office to discuss some of the sad cases Tom was working on where it was felt there had been a clear miscarriage of justice, and whilst there I was fortunate enough to meet Tom's friend Peter Benenson (the founder of Amnesty), who often popped into the office for a friendly business chat. I would make them both cups of tea with a few biscuits on a plate, which was always very much appreciated.

It was a very different atmosphere to where I had been working at the estate agents in Brighton and was able to pick up an extraordinary typing speed, which was generally remarked upon. It was on one of those occasions whilst I was tapping away that Lady Sylvia Chancellor happened to be passing by. "Oh, my dear," she said, "I have never heard anyone type so fast. It's Elizabeth, isn't it?" She had met me on a previous occasion.

Lady Chancellor had also been granted an OBE for her work connected with the Prisoners Wives Service, which she founded in 1965, understanding that families had to cope on their own when the breadwinner, being the husband and father, was condemned to prison, and did not know where to turn. The association not only gave much needed advice but also moral support to families, which helped the prisoners themselves by reassuring them that their loved ones were receiving sympathetic attention.

She was tall, slim and willowy and rocked backwards and forwards as she spoke. Her voice was gentle, often ending her sentences in a whisper. Her eyes were constantly fluttering from closed to half closed as she miraculously kept a pair of strange-looking thin-rimmed glasses balancing on the end of her nose. Her hair was blonde mixed with a few grey strands, neatly combed forward, which created a curl at the end of a long fringe that jumped around like a moving caterpillar as she carried on faffing and twittering away just for the sake of it. She was eccentric to say the least, but she was a good soul with good intentions.

Her husband, Sir Christopher Chancellor, whom she met at Cambridge University, was Chairman of the Bowater Corporation besides his role as head of the organisation Reuters. As Lady Chancellor was talking away in her usual eloquent manner she suddenly offered me a job as a shorthand secretary. "Would you like to work in Reuters?" she asked. Of course I wanted to work in Reuters. It was a wonderful opportunity and I think that Tom had something to do with it although I knew he would have preferred me to have got a job in barristers' chambers, working in the Temple. But as those positions were exceedingly rare and did not arise that often, Reuters was a second option enabling me to continue with my secretarial skills and not be out of work when his new secretary arrived.

The interview at Reuters did not take long. I entered a magnificent room, pale-green carpeted, where the deputy chairman Mr Harvey sat behind a solid oak desk with his back to a splendid bay window overlooking Fleet Street. His personal secretary – tall, slim, wearing glasses – whose desk sat in the corner of the room got up to greet me with a polite smile and asked me to sit down opposite Mr Harvey.

"Do you know Lord Chancellor?" asked Mr Harvey wistfully.

"Er, no, I don't know him," I replied. He was not expecting that answer and looking a little perplexed, starred at me over the rims of his glasses.

"Do you know Lady Chancellor"? he asked.

"Oh yes, she is a great friend of Tom's who I have met whilst working in the offices of Justice."

Mr Harvey pursed his lips as he looked again over his glasses with a twinkle in his eye. "Right," he said, "you start Monday morning, alright?"

That was the interview. I thanked him and as his secretary opened the door for me, continuing her smile, I walked out of the room.

★

I shared an office with two other shorthand typists of my own age and we had plenty of fun together, mimicking the personnel around us, sometimes sharing a sing-song of the latest hit record that had reached No.1 in the chart or helping each other decipher some of the difficult words we could not read from our shorthand notes. Windowed off were four men in the admin department sitting next door behind desks, who divided their work between us. They might have heard us in the other room but never remarked about it and never joined in.

The experience I gained from working in Reuters was invaluable not just because of the practise I had in perfecting my shorthand and typing skills but because of the interaction I shared with some of the journalists and other working colleagues in the building, who needed my assistance in helping them use some of the machinery in the office such as a Xerox photocopy machine, stencil duplicating printer and Banda, which I had been trained to utilise. Their work was generally urgent with deadlines, and my intermingling and sharing my expertise of the machines with them gave me a sense of self-confidence as they showed generous appreciation towards my help.

Typists seemed to come and go fairly frequently for some reason or another, and after having spent two years in Reuters with far more secretarial capabilities than I had when I started, Tom got in touch to say that if I was interested, there was an opportunity to work as a trainee secretary in Barristers' Chambers. I had to make a decision in a short length of time as I knew posts to work in the Temple on an admin basis were few and far between, and realising it was an opportunity not to be missed, I decided to accept the challenge by visiting Chambers for an interview.

*

I was delighted to be accepted as a trainee junior secretary to a set of barristers in Brick Court, with the assumption that if they were happy with my work, I could eventually be moved to another set when a vacancy became available in the Temple area.

The Chambers were known as Lord Devlin's Chambers, housing interesting names such as Curtis-Bennett QC, Robert

Gatehouse QC, Philip Owen QC – who was Head of Chambers – and Nicholas Lyle QC (who later became the Attorney General in John Major's Government, long after I had left the Chambers), with many other junior and senior barristers who were also accommodated in the set.

My first day was beyond comprehension. A neatly waist-coated Senior Clerk, Horace, wearing a bow tie, guided me to where I was to share a cosy room with two other experienced senior shorthand secretaries who had been there for years. A floral armchair occupied a corner of the office, surrounded by bookcases lining the walls, and I was given the desk by the window overlooking the courtyard.

Just at that moment, a rather pink-faced gentleman came running into the hallway. "Horace, Horace, where are my garters?" he asked in a petulant manner.

"I put them out for you, Sir," replied Horace obediently.

"Well, I can't find them, I can't find them," he said, getting flustered, running back and forth from the corridor to his room, where he hoped to be able to find them. I imagined that the gentleman was not particularly expecting to see anyone other than Horace the Clerk so I tried to pretend that I had not noticed anything.

I sat down at the desk that had been allotted for me, deciding to practise on the new Adler electric typewriter, when suddenly an extraordinarily handsome man wearing a silk cravat, white knee breeches and garters around the thigh wandered into the office. I could not believe what I was witnessing as he approached me in full regalia, asking if I would be good enough to type a letter for him. He must have sensed my apprehension as a kind smile slowly etched across his tanned looks whilst he placed the letter in front of me, elegantly displaying the finest of lace that was delicately attached to the cuffs of his shirt sleeves. I thought I was hallucinating, believing I was in the Dickens era, wondering if I was awake, when at that moment the clerk came back into the room, acknowledging himself.

"Ah, good morning, Sir, you've introduced yourselves. This is Mr Nicholas Lyle QC, Elizabeth. Let me take you around Chambers to meet the other members," said the clerk, and he escorted me down an elegant hallway that was laid with a dark cherry, thick pile carpet. We stopped now and again as he proudly pointed to various pictures that had been neatly placed along the walls of previous members of Chambers, QCs and Judges who had become well-known in their profession over the years. One of the doors was ajar and the clerk lightly knocked before he heard it was appropriate to enter. It opened into an exquisitely decorated room of light Wedgewood blue, facing long windows that overlooked Garden Court in the Temple. Heavy velvet curtains of a deep violet reached to the floor and swept back to let in strips of sunlight onto the plush carpet and interior of the room.

"I'm still in the state of undress," said the Head of Chambers, obviously relishing the moment but cleverly concealing his amusement. He began describing the regalia he was wearing, speaking fluidly about the historic value and dates of each piece that he was to embellish upon his person, but my mind was not focused on such detail; all I could see was a middle-aged man, fully wigged and half dressed in knee breeches, prancing around not knowing where to put his garters!

Those important bands he was to wear had been neatly laid out by the clerk on the leather winged chair for all to see, but he discreetly hoped their visibility had absconded as his intention was to let everyone understand how unfitting and awkward such garments were going to be once placed around his upper thigh, and he needed our compassion for the price he had to pay for the position he was in. Not knowing fully where to look without embarrassment, my eye eventually fell on the shiny black patent shoes he was wearing, noticing the gleaming white buckles on the front. After I remarked on their smart appearance, he haughtily replied that they were mightily uncomfortable to wear, never mind having to walk in, whereupon we all chuckled together at the difficulties he had to endure.

I honestly believed on my first day of arriving in Chambers that the dressing ceremony was a daily routine and that the barristers wore those clothes every day, until I learnt that they were privileged to wear such garments for a special occasion dating back to the middle ages, where Judges and Queen's Counsel would walk from the Royal Courts of Justice in all their regalia to Westminster Abbey for a service conducted by the Dean of Westminster. After the service, the Judges and QCs, fully robed, would carry on with their walk in public – the short distance from the Abbey to the Houses of Parliament, where the Lord Chancellor would entertain them with a 'breakfast' made up of a small buffet in the Westminster Hall.

When the group of overdressed QCs and Judges eventually left Chambers that morning to join the important procession of the day, a lone member, Walter Gumble QC, an elderly gentleman, asked me into his room to take shorthand as he wanted to dictate an urgent Statement of Claim.

He was a dour gentleman, softly spoken, very precise in his manner, telling me when he wanted a capital letter, a comma or other punctuation. He solemnly walked from one end of the room to the other in his pinstripes, nestling his arms behind his back as he carefully recited the body of the Statement in deep thought. Backwards and forwards he strolled, from one corner of the Persian carpet to the other, continually swivelling on the same spots where he had unintentionally created two very large holes in the floor covering that revealed the bare floorboards underneath, which creaked on every turn of his pivot.

Whilst working there I became fascinated by some of the characters and was inspired enough to draw a few quick pen and ink cartoon drawings of them in their wigs and gowns, and others in their bowler hats, which I was fortunate enough to sell at Sweet & Maxwell, who placed them in their shop window down Chancery Lane.

Even I became eccentric after six months or so working there, before a vacancy was advertised for a legal secretary in another set of Chambers in the Temple, Francis Taylor Buildings, and my name was put forward as a good candidate.

There were quite a few applicants applying from outside the Temple who had heard about the vacancy, but because I had been working in Lord Devlin's Chambers, my experience tipped the balance and I was offered the post.

★

My brother at that time was also taking an interest in the legal profession and attended university in London to study law whilst my mother and I moved into a spacious flat in Rochester Row, just off from Victoria Street. She got a position across the road as a senior draughtswoman, joining other civil servants at Westminster City Hall and one of the principal projects she catered for was the new Piccadilly scheme, where all her drawings had to be flawless. If her pen went through a building by mistake, she would have to start the whole drawing all over again in case the error or other mishaps were overlooked at a meeting; very exacting, painstaking work, but I believe she also felt a great sense of achievement when she had successfully completed a batch of drawings for those important meetings.

I was to start my new position at Francis Taylor Buildings in the Temple and after having moved into the new flat in London, I found it much more convenient to be able to just cross the road into Victoria Street, where I could catch the No.11 bus to Fleet Street, without having to travel by train from Brighton every day.

I was to be the only secretary working for sixteen barristers and two QCs, which sounded a lot of people to work for but was not unusual for Barristers' Chambers, and as they found tapes more appropriate to use than the taking down of shorthand notes, it automatically saved everyone an awful lot of time.

The senior clerk, Bernard, introduced me to the Head of Chambers, Mr Edward Gardner QC, who was also a Tory MP for Billericay and South Fylde. He emphasised emphatically that it was his dog who had won most of the votes, having gained an overwhelming majority of 36,000, which was a landslide result at the time.

During the Second World War he survived the sinking of two ships, and in 1945 he was appointed as a commander in the Royal Naval Volunteer Reserve (RNVR) and Chief of Naval Information. He was a mighty man with an emulating presence, taking the stage, powerfully built but friendly, with blue twinkling eyes that shone with life. I found I did not do a lot of work for him as he already had a personal parliamentary secretary in the House of Commons who had looked after him for many years, but when he attended Chambers, on the odd occasion, it was my responsibility to make sure that his work was put before everyone else's.

Bernard then introduced me to Evelyn Monier-Williams (known as Bill), Deputy Head of Chambers, sitting behind a large desk piled high with books whilst busily working on papers. The moment he looked at me with his deep, dark brown eyes, I knew he was the man I had met in my out-of-body experience when I was fourteen years old, the man standing by the car smiling at me on my descent back into my body. He looked older than he appeared in that experience as his silky white hair flopped occasionally to one side of his face, but the drawing I had sketched of him that next morning after my experience was identical – the same eyes, expression and aura. It was like an electric current had jumped right through me and as Bernard introduced us, Bill looked at me giving me a slight smile and I wondered if he felt the same.

When we left the room, Bernard told me that Bill was instrumental in the posthumous reinstatement to the Bar of Mahatma Gandhi, who was once a law student at the Inner Temple during the years 1888–1891 and who was expelled in 1922 after his campaign of non-cooperation with the British authorities and subsequent imprisonment. Bernard reiterated that Bill played a big part in restoring Ghandi's reputation, adding that he felt it was a very honourable thing to do.

After meeting other senior members of the Bar, Bernard showed me where I would be sitting, which was amongst the clerks in their room overlooking the Temple Church with its pretty little garden in the foreground.

It was a lovely spot, but I likened sitting in the clerks' room to sitting in a bus station with the door continually swinging, back and forth as clients arrived with their solicitors for conferences all day. There were deliveries of the post, bundles of papers and briefs from articled clerks; the phone was constantly ringing; and there were barristers popping in and out at every available moment to check with the clerks when they would next be appearing in court. With all the noise and chaos around me, I found it very difficult to hear the tapes or concentrate properly on the volumes of work I had to get through for all the barristers there and felt it necessary to discuss the problems I was having with Bernard and the other clerks to see what could be done. But I was disappointed with their reaction as it became apparent that they were not interested in the slightest with my difficulties, showing their attitude to be 'take it or leave it', and in the end I had no alternative but to involve a member of Chambers and asked to speak to Bill, the Deputy Head of Chambers, about my problems.

He invited me into his large office overlooking Mitre Court and asked me to sit down at his desk opposite him to explain what was troubling me, whilst giving me the assurance that whatever I told him would be in the strictest confidence. I found him to be very understanding, listening intently, and after he considered everything I had to say, I was relieved to hear him reassure me that he would try to do everything that he could to resolve the matter. I left his room feeling a weight had been lifted from my shoulders, although I had no idea what he could do about the matter – particularly without causing animosity amongst the clerks, who I thought might resent the fact that I had gone over their heads and thereby could deliberately cause me to feel uncomfortable whilst working there.

After a lot of discussion amongst the barristers, who came up with all sorts of proposals as space was very tight in Chambers (with rooms sometimes being shared between three, especially amongst the junior counsel), I never believed there could be an answer or that there would be an easy solution to the problem, but as Bill had reassured me that he would do all he could to sort something out for me, I waited patiently in anticipation.

It was finally agreed by Chambers, that one of the larger loos overlooking the Temple Church, with frosted windows, could be ripped out and made into a little typing room for my use, which sounded a splendid idea, but before any changes could take place, it was necessary to obtain authority from the Treasury Office that such works could go ahead.

Whilst another party having to be involved in the agreement of any repairs to take place within Chambers might have been a disabling factor, I was told by one of the barristers that Bill had recently been elected Master Bencher at the Treasury Office, which opened up a completely new aspect to the situation. It meant that Bill was perfectly placed to play a major role in persuading the other members on the bench to agree Chambers' proposals, and my hopes were certainly raised when I heard that news.

Before matters could progress, proposals had to be put in writing and a letter needed to be typed for the Treasury office, laying out the explanations why, members of Chambers had agreed for the necessity of the secretary to have her own separate office away from the Clerks' room and why building works should go ahead.

Bill walked into the Clerks' room and quietly placed the letter on my desk ready for typing. As he did so, I could sense the clerks' apprehension about why things were swaying in my direction, and their wondering why I was getting preferential treatment, especially as I always got a lovely smile from Bill when he happened to walk in the room.

It was not too long afterwards when I heard that the Treasury Office had given their full consent for the refurbishment of the washroom to be made into a small office for human use. Thus, the work could begin.

★

Whilst works were being organised to redesign my little room in Chambers, I took the opportunity of going on holiday with my mother and brother. We decided to go somewhere different from the usual holiday resorts and were one of the first groups of tourists allowed to enter Russia in 1968.

My father kindly gave us a lift to Tilbury Docks in London with all our suitcases for the early morning sail, where we embarked on a Russian cruise ship named *Baltika*. My mother and I shared a two-berth cabin and my brother shared with another gentleman travelling on his own. We waved at my father, standing with a few other onlookers, as the ship slowly left the dock until we finally set sail.

Our first stop was Copenhagen, where we were able to disembark from the ship to take photos of the Little Mermaid, visit the Tivoli Gardens and wander around the shops before returning to the ship for the evening sail to Helsinki, Finland. The waters were very calm as we arrived in the port of Helsinki, and we spent a day exploring the city, travelling on trams and visiting housing complexes with wondrous fountains and picturesque lakes, and little islands with not more than one or two houses built where the neighbours owned boats to island hop rather than a car in the garage. On returning to the ship, we knew the next stop would be Russia. We were to arrive in Leningrad, as it was called before changing its name to St Petersburg on September 6th, 1991.

As we were sailing into Russia, the ship steered us through miles of manmade strips of land that guided us into the country. It was getting dark by then and a damp fog had gently surrounded us by the time we had disembarked from the ship onto land. Customs were heavily guarded as our belongings were checked and scrutinised before we were allowed to step foot into the country. The streets were poorly lit, dour and dank as we boarded the coach that took us from the port to our hotel in the centre of Leningrad, Hotel Ukraine. During the journey the coach stopped as there appeared to be a fist fight between two men, blocking the road. It was difficult to see as the lighting was faint, but there was a sense of apprehension amongst everyone, including the driver. Fortunately, the coach restarted and we eventually arrived at the hotel before midnight but too late for dinner. The staff kindly offered us a sandwich and a hot lemon tea. A live band was playing 1940s music in a separate room adjacent to where we were sitting in the dining room, which had high ceilings and chandeliers, where we watched men in full uniform dancing with their partners to what sounded like old wartime music. It all felt so surreal, like living in another era – the way they were dressed, their hairstyles and the music.

Later, we were shown to our rooms, which were sparse with no en-suite toilets, which meant we had to walk down a long corridor and then down another to where an elderly lady, dressed in what looked like peasant clothing was seated on a wooden chair outside the bathroom area, offering pieces of paper for our use. The indignity of the whole process took a while to get used to, to say the least. Another discrepancy was that there was no plug attached to the bath; it was left to the discretion of the visitor to bring their own, which had not been explained properly before the trip. Whether it was a deliberate attempt to save on water, I had no idea, but the only way around it was to borrow from other tourists who were wise enough to bring one with them.

The next morning, we were introduced to our guide Natasha, who was to take us on organised trips to visit some of the landmarks that we had all heard about, the first being the Hermitage, one of the largest and most prestigious museums in the world, exhibiting everything from impressionist masterpieces to fascinating oriental treasurers, with over three million items in its collection. It is estimated that you would need eleven years to view each exhibit on display for just one minute, so it's best to organise beforehand what one wishes to focus on.

We found we were restricted from walking anywhere without our guide Natasha, a tall blonde woman who seemed to know the answers to all our questions, reciting them in beautiful English. But I noticed she never smiled. Her cheeks were white, showing no expression. She never shared a joke or laughed with us, or blushed or grimaced when we tried to communicate with her, and we felt blocked from being able to get to know her personally, but she was highly professional in her duties as a guide, which we all remarked upon.

After the Hermitage we were taken towards St Isaac's Cathedral, which dominates the Russian skyline with its ecclesiastical architecture, built in 1818 by Emperor Alexander I and completed in 1858 by his younger brother, Emperor Nicholas I, who died six weeks after it was completed. The facades are decorated with sculptures and massive granite columns whilst the interior acquired nine hundred pounds of gold, sixteen tons of malachite, 1,100 pounds of lapis lazuli and 1,000 tons of bronze. So much wealth.

Natasha took us down the Nevsky Prospekt, being the main high street in St Petersburg – or Leningrad, as it was known then – and as I was used to wearing make-up with a prominent lipstick, a lot of people pointed to their lips as we passed by. Cosmetics were a luxury and not easy to get hold of throughout Russia in 1967 – as with other goods, for which they had to queue for hours outside empty shelved shops just to meet their basic needs.

Strangely, we did not see any animals; no dogs on leads with their owners, no cats prowling around. There were no children alongside their parents or babies in prams. The streets were empowered by adults mainly walking on their own, having worked for hours in factories and other industries and transferred after work towards the colleges or school groups, where they took on extra lessons to study other pursuits. Travel by bus and tube was all one price – two kopeks (approximately two pence in UK coinage) to wherever you wanted to go – and easy to sort out at the ticket office.

Along the pavement we came across the occasional stall, selling sweets costing one kopek each and ice creams in tiny cones. The other stalls sold cigarettes, which could be bought individually, mainly made up of an empty cardboard tube with the tip containing the tobacco – the opposite as to how we knew an ordinary cigarette, where the lengthy tubular shape contains the tobacco and the tip is made up of cellulose acetate (a plastic) packed tightly together to create a filter. Even though the tobacco in a Russian cigarette was limited in its length, it was not limited in its strength, and it was wise to smoke it in small doses.

Early in the morning you would see droves of people travelling to work and amongst the crowds, were men and women carrying wicker baskets filled with mushrooms that they had spent hours picking from the local forests. Apparently, picking mushrooms was a loved Russian pastime handed down from generation to generation, which they either sold to the hotels or used for their own consumption.

All our meals were organised from the hotels as there were no restaurants at that time, and what I found amusing was being served soup after the main course. Strangely enough, it worked well – instead of having soup before a main meal, which often satisfied one's appetite, and having soup as a second course helped with the digestion.

One of the most beautiful places we visited was the Peterhof Palace, not far from Pushkin Village, built in 1703 by Peter the Great – a series of palaces and gardens located in Petergorf, whose golden domes gleamed in the sun. The ornate gates opened into avenues of lime trees and the gardens contained three thundering waterfalls, sixty-seven fountains and thirty-seven statues covered in gold leaf, and no expense of lives was spared in making it a reality. It was opulence itself and the lay-man felt privileged to be able to enjoy the gardens that were once enjoyed by those who believed they belonged to the elite.

After a week of sightseeing, we travelled on the overnight train from Leningrad to Moscow, taking eight hours to arrive at 8.30 the next morning. The views from the train at night were vast and intimidating: miles and miles of open land with hardly any lighting. We tried to get a short nap, putting our heads down on makeshift beds – flat boards, one on top of the other – as the train rolled from side to side without disturbance on its long journey. We arrived in Moscow on time at 8.30am and the moment we set foot off the train, I could not believe I was seeing women in boiler suits on the building sites, carrying heavy loads and climbing scaffolding just like the men.

Another female guide, Alexandra collected us from the station, where a coach was waiting to take us to Hotel Kiefskaya. After a welcome breakfast she took us on a walk around the Red Square, including the well-known GUM store, (now serving as a shopping mall) but was then the main state trading department store of the former Soviet Union, which we found extraordinary as there were only a few items on display for sale. We took umpteen pictures of the delightful Basil Church with its picturesque Byzantine dome, built in 1552 when Ivan the Terrible commissioned the landmark church – officially the Intercession Cathedral – to commemorate his victory when he captured the stronghold of Kazan.

There was a long queue to see Lenin lying in state, which the guide told us started from the very early hours in the morning, and as it would have been a long wait we decided not to take part but instead witnessed the changing of the guard, which we felt was a poignant moment to experience: three Russian Kremlin guards, their faces sombre, standing to attention in honour of the Unknown Soldier, where there had been an eternal flame burning since 1967, lit by Leonid Brezhnev, to commemorate eleven million soldiers lost in the Second World War, ten million wounded, and one million disabled, besides ten million civilians killed. On the hour, every hour, on the single gongs of the Kremlin Clock – called Kuranti, on Spasskaya Tower – three soldiers march out from the Kremlin to replace the two soldiers already guarding the tomb, with a single soldier returning to the Kremlin. It is an impressive sight in all its simplicity with its perfect synchronised movement, straight-legged but high-stepped in unbashful pomp and ceremony.

We had a punishing schedule for the next day, when we were taken by coach to visit Yasnaya Polyana, Tolstoy's house, where we had to remove our shoes and wear flat slippers. We shuffled around the floorboards of his cottage, finding his study, where a modest desk showed us where he wrote his classics *War and Peace* and *Anna Karenin*. Ink pots and quills were left as they were, overlooking an amazing view of hills and trees from his window, giving us a glimpse of how it was in his day.

The next morning we visited Lenin's museum, where his clothes were on display showing the holes made by the bullets he had encountered, and at the Baltika, a ship museum, we saw garments worn by Catherine the Great. She was such a tiny lady with the smallest of waists. It was when I saw the studs of exquisite jewels notched into the stirrups of the horses that I envisaged wealth being carelessly paraded through the streets of Russia – where there was so much poverty amongst the ordinary people, with children running around barefoot, unable to afford shoes in the harshest of winters – and it became apparent how a Revolution could take place. Afterwards we were rushed back to the Hotel Kiefskaya in Moscow to have something to eat before changing to see the ballet that night at the Palace of Congress. Such a thrill.

We returned to Leningrad on the overnight train, staying at the Hotel Astoria before returning to Tilbury, England. My mother took a terrible risk in hiding a rouble in her bra. I cannot explain the nerves she must have felt in doing so because if she had been caught the consequences could have been devastating, and I could never imagine the repercussions. Everything was checked before we were allowed out of the country, including all the notes and coins in our purses, but she got away with it; such a relief. After getting a chain down Shepherd Market in London, we made it into a pendant which became one of my most beloved items of jewellery, that I wear to this day.

★

Russia was a wonderful experience and I felt exhilarated from the holiday, besides being separated from the clerks for a while, and when I returned to Chambers two weeks later, Bill was waiting to show me my new room, decorated and equipped with everything I would need as a secretary. I was delighted to see the transformation.

The little office was glorious. I overlooked the Temple Church, which gave a sense of serenity as I gazed in awe at the elegant stained glass windows, where rays shone from the precious pieces of coloured pane that glinted in the sunlight. The garden was like a haven of peace away from the hustle and bustle of Fleet Street nearby, and a pink magnolia tree blossomed in the spring, charming the little iron gate that locked the quaint private garden from public view. The Temple Church was built in the twelfth century by the Knights Templar and underneath the garden was the crypt where Bill's father lay, once Head of Chambers in Paper Buildings, besides having been a Master Bencher in the Treasury Office himself.

There were Victorian gas lamps in the Temple up until 1976 and I was fortunate enough to watch a lone lamplighter, wearing a long mac with a cap on his head, climb a ladder at dusk to light the lamp by hand. The timing was scheduled to fit in with the changing twilight darkness of the evening and the lamps had been deliberately placed to light up some of the concealed alcoves and steps that are part of the precincts of the Temple. In the winter it was magical when it snowed, to watch the flakes gently pass the lit glass of the old gas lamp. It was like going back in time, something special and quaint, matching the area that had a mediaeval feel to it. When the lamplighter finished one lamp, he gathered his tool kit and carried it with his ladder to the next lamp and started the whole process over again.

On another occasion, one day in the summer, when my window was wide open, the Dean from the church came out to water his flowers, as he often did, and I asked him why he was carefully watering a ping pong ball on the soil every day, which looked like it had been left there by mistake. He laughed and said that it was a white mushroom. As the weeks and months went by, I saw how the ping pong ball grew to the size of a tennis ball, and it was only then that I began to believe him!

*

After the first six months or so, whilst I was enjoying my new little office, Tom was organising his annual Justice Ball at the Savoy Hotel and asked me to try and sell some tickets in Chambers.

I was not finding it easy, but a young man, Malcolm – an articled clerk who often delivered briefs from his firm of solicitors – happened to overhear about the tickets and surprised me by offering to buy one, but only if I allowed him to escort me. It was an offer I could not refuse as I needed a partner to accompany me, even though he reminded me in looks of Rob, my first date, the young fellow I had met at the estate agents in Brighton, but I did not want to allow that to stop my accepting his offer.

Malcolm collected me. He looked so smart, wearing a black tuxedo topped off with a black velvet bow tie. I wore a long black taffeta dress with small straps lowered off the shoulders, shaped at the front to hide cleavage, with a bare back, and I held a tiny evening bag made of silver sequins. My jewellery and watch were expensive and feminine in style. I wore a silver locket around my neck and I left my hair long with a fringe. I felt excited. It was my first ball.

We arrived at the back of the Savoy on the embankment side of the building, where cars and taxis accumulated to let out their guests. Women wore long elegant dresses with expensive stoles wrapped around their shoulders; some wore elbow-length gloves. They held petite evening bags and had strings of pearls around their necks, with their hair neatly swept up onto their heads, gathered by a hairclip, sparkling with diamonds. Most of the men wore tuxedos and tailsuits, and some docked their top hats as they entered the hotel with all the pandemonium of the ushers, who were eager to make sure everyone was looked after whilst discreetly checking their tickets.

Lord and Lady Shawcross were waiting in the foyer to greet the guests as they arrived and shook hands with them as their names were called out. Malcolm and I were not left out. Afterwards we were ushered through into the dining area, passing flunkies along the way, who were standing to attention in the corridors. They were dressed in full regalia and wearing powdered wigs, not blinking an eye, pretending that this was an everyday occurrence as the guests leisurely floated around them.

The lavish dining room, with its high ceilings, had been arranged like a royal banquet with long hanging chandeliers that glittered down onto immaculately laid round tables. The cutlery gleamed on the starched white tablecloths. Fancy matching napkins had been neatly placed against the wine and drinking glasses that were waiting for the guests as they slowly strolled into the dining area. Bouquets of fresh flowers had been carefully placed in the centre of each table, giving off a wonderful aroma as we tried to find our names that were printed on cards to show us where we were supposed to be seated. Malcolm and I found our spot fairly quickly and we sat down on plush red-cushioned seats to watch the others slowly take their places.

Then, out of the blue, Bill from my Chambers greeted me and introduced himself around the table before taking his place, sitting next to me on my left, with Malcom on my right.

Everyone at the table slowly got to know one another as Bill automatically found himself heading the table, taking the stage as he captivated the attention of everyone around him, sharing his tales and keeping them amused. The waiters began to pour out the champagne, that sparkled in the glasses around the table while we waited for the twelve-course menu to begin. The toing and froing of the smartly dressed waiters appeared endless, and there was a constant flow of exquisitely decorated dishes, light and simple, each one discussed at great measure whilst Bill enlightened us about some of the traditions of a full course menu. To finish there was brandy, coffee and cigars if so desired.

At one point, as I was trying to get a word in amongst the bevy of guests who were monopolising Bill with their questions, I suddenly felt a hand gently touch my bare back. It did not last long – a couple of seconds – but it was enough to send an excited shiver down my spine as I knew it was not Malcolm's.

After dinner, Bill slipped away, and Malcolm and I were left to enjoy the rest of the evening, dancing to the live band which played a varied selection of music, that we could all enjoy. It was like a magical dream that I never wanted to end.

In the early hours of the morning, Malcolm and I finally left the hotel to walk along the embankment, slightly disorientated and very overdressed, with our faces aglow, not caring how we must have looked as the early morning traffic passed by.

Yes, I had a hangover the next day, but I felt it was worth it.

★

When I got back to Chambers a day later, there was a lot of work piled high in the trays waiting for me in my office and I checked through to see if there was anything urgent that needed to be done straight away.

Since I had my own room, I often worked late, not only to

earn the extra overtime as an added bonus at the end of the month, but to catch up with the junior barristers' workload, as their briefs were generally put at the back of the queue during the day by the more senior barristers, whose work was always looked upon as priority.

As Bill regularly dined at the Inns of Court in the heart of the Temple, returning to Chambers late in the evening, he would often pop his head around the door to say hello and see how I was. On those occasions he would stop to talk for a while and I learnt a lot about him. He was educated at Charterhouse and then read history at University College, Oxford. When the war broke out, he was awarded with a war degree before serving as a Field Gunner Officer with the 8th Army and later with the 50th Northumbrian Division. While in Tunisia he took part in the Battle of the Mareth Line, and he told me he was deeply affected by the experience. The war took him to North Africa, Sicily, France, the Low Countries and Germany, where he was stationed in the Rhineland and organised the re-opening of the local theatre there, where he met his German wife – an opera singer – by putting on general entertainment for the British troops who were waiting to be demobbed after the war.

He was a good-looking man with twinkling dark brown eyes that seemed to delve into my soul as he spoke, and even though he had a confident air about him, I sensed he had a depth and empathy, unlike the others. We shared stories about ourselves and when he recognised my beliefs, he took the courage to tell me that whilst he was a student involved in the Oxford Union, he became interested in the Spiritualist movement and followed Madame Blavatsky, a Russian occultist medium and philosopher who co-founded the Theosophical Society in 1875.

He then told me that he often sensed his father around him and explained a difficult incident that happened whilst he was in court, where his voice changed dramatically when addressing the jury and he knew he had been taken over by his deceased father without warning, making it difficult to finish his summing up, whereupon the court had to be adjourned early that day. He wanted to reiterate that it had only happened the once but that was enough to keep him on the alert for any future manifestations. He chuckled about it in humour, looking back, saying he did not share that side of himself with the rest of his family or with his colleagues in Chambers.

It made us very close.

Over the months, we got to know each other very well and it was not long after when one night he arrived back in Chambers late after dining, I made him a cup of tea which I took into his room. He was standing by his library of law books, contemplating which one was necessary to read for his case the next morning. After I had laid the cup and saucer on his desk, I looked over at him and he at me, and with nothing said between us, we approached each other and kissed.

We fell in love. It was one of those things. He was much older than me, but that did not matter.

★

During that time my mother married for the second time to an author, Frank Cousins, who was also a Fellow of the Royal Astronomical Society, having written books on the subject – *Sundials* and *The Solar System* – besides lecturing guide tours at the Planetarium in London. The timing of their marriage seemed right as I was ready to move out of the Rochester Row household and I found a little flat to live in Highgate.

The liaison between Bill and I remained blissful for over three years, but in the middle of our relationship he became one of the youngest appointed Circuit Judges at the age of forty-eight, which automatically created difficulties between us, particularly in finding the time to meet up as we had done when he was tenanted in Chambers.

On the day of his inauguration, not wanting to be noticed by the other barristers, I hid behind a tree in the precincts of the Temple courtyard to witness his grand arrival, which was due around midday. He knew where I would be standing as I had mentioned what I would be doing the day before, joking with him that if he held the bottom of his new long wig, it meant he loved me.

A Bentley eventually entered the main gates of the Temple and parked outside Chambers. The chauffeur went to open the door for Bill, who was having some difficulty due to the heavy robes he was wearing, and one of the clerks who had been patiently waiting for his arrival immediately went to his aid to help him out of the car. A lone photographer who had been commissioned to take photographs of the event was focusing on various angles to take a collection of pictures of Bill as he placed himself at the side of the car, standing proudly in all his regalia. Then he held the bottom part of his wig, knowing I was in the distance, which I immediately recognised as the portrayal of that same image I saw during my out-of-body experience when I was fourteen. It was a strange moment, as though time was limitless and I could not understand the meaning behind it.

Soon after, Bill left his tenancy in Chambers, as was customary for a Judge, making the place feel very empty without him. I began to miss his company during the day, having enjoyed the casual ability to meet and chat with him as we had done over the years. It was also impossible for him to call me as the clerks would have answered the main switchboard, wondering why I should have a personal call from him especially as he had become a Judge and left Chambers. He also gradually declined from entering Chambers in the evening after dining, knowing it would have looked out of place unless for a specific reason or for a deliberate intention of meeting another member there and it became more and more problematic for us to keep in touch with one another. Nonetheless, we carried on meeting each other for another year in that restrictive way, after he had left Chambers.

I was able to capture a picture of him dressed in his full regalia whilst walking in the Judges' Procession past the Abbey on his way to the Lord Chancellor's 'breakfast' at the Houses of Parliament, holding the bottom of his wig as he spotted me in front of a group of people who had gathered together to watch the procession pass by. He looked so distinguished in his purple robes.

Watching him in all his grandeur, now a Judge having reached the pinnacle of his career, I reluctantly began to see that our friendship could never return to what it was.

Soon after the procession, my mother phoned to say that she had received a disturbing call from Bill's wife, who was difficult to understand at first with her broken English and German accent but said that she kept repeating the same words over and over, "How dare your daughter be going out with my huzzband?" – so much so that my mother replied, "How dare your husband be going out with my daughter!" after which it appeared the caller put the phone down on her.

Bill once told me that we had a very close and deep bond which was difficult to explain to the outside world, and it was disturbing to hear that his wife had personally phoned my mother to complain, especially as I believed she had always known about our liaison from the beginning and had not previously shown any signs of caring one way or the other. But now that she was portrayed as a Judge's wife, perhaps she felt the need to necessitate the security of her position, finding it difficult to accept the connection that Bill and I felt for one another.

It was not long after the call when it was agreed that Bill and his wife visit my mother and stepfather at Rochester Row, without my presence, to calm the situation down. My mother explained what happened, as I recall. Apparently, Bill confessed that he had fallen head over heels in love with me, after which his wife got up from her chair and stood in the middle of the room aghast, saying, "In that case, why don't you divorze me then?" Bill explained to my parents, in front of his wife, that one of the main reasons he had fallen for me was the fact that we had never committed adultery.

It was not an easy time and with Bill's family and other members of the Chambers already knowing about our relationship, with all the controversy surrounding it, I started to feel isolated in my little room as there was no-one there I could talk to. One day merged into the next and with the weight of the anxieties taking their toll, I started to realise that there could never be a future in it.

My brother too had just left university having passed his Bar exam and was about to start his pupillage in a set of Chambers in the Temple nearby. Knowing that barristers were a magnet of information between Chambers, I became concerned for his reputation as some members might have heard about his sister going out with a Judge, which might not have gone down too well at the start of his career with colleagues not fully understanding the true nature of our relationship.

Realising the difficulties that lay ahead and accepting that the relationship had come to an end, with a very heavy heart, I finally made the drastic decision to leave Chambers, without having another job to go to.

The next day everything felt black. I could not see a future. All I wanted to do was run away from lawyers and the memories connected with them.

However, the agencies kept ringing and begging me to return to legal work as they said it was where my experience lay, and eventually, in time, I agreed to temp for a legal agency, where I was sent out to solicitors in Central London. It was a varied lifestyle and I travelled to different parts of the capital, met many people and gained experience from different aspects of the law, and after many years of visiting a varied selection of solicitors in central London, I finally settled with the firm of Gregory Rowcliffe & Co. in Holborn, where I felt I could be reasonably happy and stayed there for over five years.

*

"It's urgent," repeated my boss, as the water kept dripping from my umbrella, creating a pool of water around my feet. He wanted his work there and then.

One dreary long day followed another, when a friend of mine, Colin, phoned to suggest a trip to Morocco on my fortnight's summer break and, finding the idea far too tempting to ignore, we decided to book the holiday together.

I had known Colin for about eighteen months after we had met waiting at a bar in a pub, The Cittie Yorke, along Holborn High Road when it was our turn to get the drinks for our colleagues, who were celebrating Christmas. He was on a six-month contract for a firm of architects as a draftsman, and as my mother was senior draftswoman at The Westminster City Hall down Victoria Street, we had something in common to discuss, keeping each other company whilst waiting for the bar staff to catch our eye. I found him easy to talk to straight away, sharing the same humour, and we decided to swap telephone numbers. Thereafter we became great friends.

When the time came to pack my suitcase, I did not know which was more exciting, the freedom from the rat race or travelling abroad again, but it did not seem to matter as the two reasons fused into one and I was ready for a change of scenery from the office.

I had visited Tangier, Morocco, many years before as a child with my parents, and knew roughly what to expect, whereas Colin had not experienced much travelling abroad and it would be his first visit to northern Africa and a Muslim country.

We booked a hotel in Agadir that looked good on paper but after arriving, we found it was located next door to a mosque, which chanted prayers three or four times in the night by loudspeaker, keeping us awake and destroying our night's sleep. We tried to change our hotel to a quieter location but being peak of the season, we soon found that it was difficult to organise and patiently waited for a vacancy in another vicinity.

We were not having much luck but strangely, by the second week of the holiday, we found we were sleeping right through the wailing of the prayers, which reminded me of when I became accustomed to the noises of the wind around our house in Rottingdean. This caused us to think twice as we liked the rooms that had been allotted to us and as we were happy with the staff at the hotel, we decided to remain where we were for the rest of our stay there.

In the first week of our holiday we organised a few trips, one of which was a coach trip to Marrakech through the Atlas Mountains. It was not as barren as expected as we often passed small groups of Bedouin by the roadside with their few camels and small herds of goats, who took their pitch at different locations in and around the desert.

After a few hours travelling in the hot sun we took a welcome stop at a remote village high up in the mountains, where camels and donkeys were used for their main source of transport and goats and chickens wandered around as they pleased. Their tents were made from camel fleece. They were dextrous people from the Berber tribe and even though they appeared poor to us, their faces shone with a certain serenity, showing a contentment money could not buy.

It was a welcome stop and we enjoyed a refreshing mint tea

and a visit to the rather primitive toilets before we boarded the coach again.

Hours later we arrived at the Palace of Tombs outside the main town centre of Marrakech, where little boys rushed to hold our hands to escort us to the outside of the Palace. They were very friendly and one little boy said he would meet me when I came out the other side.

The Palace was equipped with marble floors and the Queen's rooms were surrounded by beautiful mosaic walls and ceilings, telling us stories of times long ago, that overlooked a forecourt where she would have been entertained by musicians, jugglers and dancers. The guide kept shouting 'step, step' emphatically as tourists were idly looking around, wandering from room to room without focusing on their footing and in jeopardy of easily tripping on the unlevel ground.

When Colin and I emerged from the Palace grounds, the little boy who had approached me earlier was still waiting patiently for us and dutifully led us back to the bus, but he got swallowed up by the other boys begging for dirhams and the guide ushered us on to the coach in a hurry.

The trip had already taken over five hours and even though it was still early morning, it was remarkably hot at 36°C as we arrived in the main town of Marrakech. The driver of the coach managed to manoeuvre his vehicle down the narrowest of alleyways where we believed people lived behind high walls, with one or two small shops displaying food outside, allowing the flies to accumulate in their droves, leaving the fruit looking as though it could do with a good wash. The buildings had a hue of red about them against beautiful blue skies, and were surrounded by dusty roads where donkey-drawn carts were the main form of transport, with a strange mix of Honda motorbikes hooting and whizzing around haphazardly in all different directions. There was a buzz about the place and a sense of fervour, but with a strong medieval essence about it that lingered in every street corner.

It was such a relief to leave the coach, ready for a walkabout, and the guide advised all the tourists to stick together as it was very easy to get lost in the alleyways of the medina. As we started on our journey he tried to stop the boys from pestering us for dirhams, telling us to link hands to make a chain so that we could not stray from the group. Colin and I found ourselves at the end of the queue and as the group were walking quickly without stopping, we were finding it difficult to keep up with those at the front. Our guide led us through dirty alleyways, passing stores filled to the brim with a variety of wares. Shops full of pottery, lanterns and leather bags, all in varying colours, shapes and designs, next to shops filled with brass ornaments piled high to the ceiling. In one of the shops, the owner banged loudly on a brass plate to show us how robust it was. His assistant came up to me to ask how much I would pay for it, but I could not stop as we were whisked through hand in hand, passing boutiques filled to the brim with djellabas, old cameras for sale, watches and jewellery, with people shouting in Arabic all around us.

Colin and I continued having trouble keeping up at the end of the queue, finding the guide was moving too fast for us, when suddenly we found ourselves separated from the group, making us feel somewhat vulnerable and not knowing where to go. A young boy came up to us whom we recognised as being the same boy who met us outside the Palace of Tombs earlier. "I'll lead you back to the coach depot," he said in broken English and, not having a choice, we had to trust him to get us back to the group. He led us through the alleyways of the market, which we could not recognise or know whether we had been through before, but we kept up with the boy, relying on his knowledge of the area to lead us back into safety. There was a tenseness in the atmosphere as we shuffled through the cobbled streets, sometimes overwhelmed with the heavy smell of incense that dulled our senses as we nervously followed the boy who kept waving and shouting 'this way'. A little lady with a veil came up to me begging for dirhams for a white hat she had knitted. I could not stop and I felt so sorry I could not help her. Loud Arabic music was playing from some of the shops from one alleyway to another until we finally emerged in the main epicentre of the market, which was overflowing with chattels, people and animals.

Suddenly, to my astonishment we saw a snake charmer with a group of people encircled around him, mesmerised by the sight, but we had only waited a few minutes before we were asked for money. The boy begged us not to hang around but to carry on and follow him. We passed a mountain of false teeth for sale. It was such a macabre sight. I just took a quick look at the horror of it, hoping I would not need the dentist whilst on holiday. Then, suddenly, we found ourselves face to face with a donkey wearing a bright red hat that had holes made for its ears, but the owner kept harassing us, begging for dirhams in exchange for pictures to be taken, whether we wanted the picture to be taken or not. As we could not stay, we hurriedly left the scene, following the boy as best we could and unexpectedly found ourselves amongst heavy crowds that had encircled as onlookers around groups of musicians playing Arabic music, but the boy got agitated with us, pleading with us to carry on following him until he finally led us towards the coach depot, where we immediately recognised other tourists from our group, who looked pleased to see us as the guide had been concerned about our disappearance and showed genuine relief to find that we were safe and sound.

We thanked the boy by giving him some dirhams but as we got on the coach to wave to him, we saw older boys circulating around him, trying to take his money. There was nothing we could do as the coach began to set off on its way. Somehow, we saw the little boy had freed himself from the group and he began running alongside the bus. All the passengers on the coach noticed how bravely he fought the crowds on the way, frantically running to keep up with us. The bus finally came to a stop fifteen minutes later, arriving at the hotel where we were staying. To our surprise, we saw the boy was already there, waiting outside, begging for dirhams. Colin and I got out of the coach and the boy started to cry, telling us that the bigger boys had taken his money and he had nothing left. Tears filled my eyes as I dipped into my purse to find some more money for him, which I placed in his tiny palm. As I did, his wet shiny cheeks slowly cracked into a beautiful smile across his face, radiating happiness and thanks as we hugged and parted good friends.

★

It was a wonderful holiday – sandy beaches, hot sun, good food and a complete rest from the job that I found so stressful in London. Colin sold me many times to shopkeepers for two or three or more camels, which I did not know he had, and we both laughed every time we left a shop as though it was the first time we had heard the joke.

At the end of the holiday we managed to put our hands in our pockets towards a special evening at the five-star Sahara Hotel along the beach, as we heard it was the place to go if one could afford it.

We took our time getting ready, making sure we looked the part. Colin wore a pale grey suit with a pastoral pink and blue tie, which suited him and I decided on a simple black dress with a colourful shawl around my shoulders in case it got chilly later at night walking along the beach on our return back to the hotel.

When we first arrived at the Sahara, we could hear the

relaxing, dulcet tones of an ornamental fountain, surrounded by miniature palm trees, perfectly placed as a centre-piece in the reception area, where the hotel concierge greeted us with a smile, showing us the directions to where we needed to go. We walked through the magnificent marble corridors, passing picturesque gardens along the way, and finally arrived at the splendid dining hall.

Beautiful plush carpets weaved by the local Berber community adorned the surrounding walls and floors in all their splendour and many soft cushions were thrown on comfortable leather sofas, which created a cosiness that warm fabrics can achieve. Glittering chandeliers twinkled as they covered the ceiling to finish off the wonderment of the luscious surroundings, taking our breath away. All the while, immaculately dressed waiters – tall, dark and handsome, wearing fezzes, harem pants (baggy trousers that we knew as Egyptian) and bright red waistcoats – elegantly carried scorching tajines containing piping hot delicious food to the customers who were patiently waiting for their orders. Each clay vessel that held sliced chicken breast mixed with vegetables as the main ingredients with spices, nuts, apricots and dates, topped with potato had slowly cooked for hours. The waiters carefully positioned the dishes on the brass tables, cautiously avoiding the fresh roses that had been meticulously placed in the centre of the tables earlier that day.

*This is the life,* both Colin and I thought as we basked in the affluence and lush surroundings of that beautiful place whilst the aroma of the mouth-watering food overtook our senses as we tucked into our tajines.

After we finished our meal, we sat back to enjoy a glass of wine together, happily observing the elegance of how the waiters ceremoniously carried their trays back and forth by lightly resting them on their shoulders, when our attention was drawn by a scurry of activity as groups of Arabic men in full djellabah started to accumulate, proudly sauntering around, taking their time, without a care in the world. We watched in amusement as about forty of them bantered with one another, some groups getting more argumentative than others, often heightening in tempo, and we wished we knew what they were saying to one another. After a while most of them had quietened down but some were still muttering under their breath as though they had not finished what they wanted to say. When all the chatter had subsided, they sat down in the form of an orchestra, where they practised a spell of tuning their instruments. Then, when they were ready, they played the most melodious Arabic music I had ever heard.

Colin and I carried on enjoying the wine, listening to the music, when to our amazement a Berber dancer appeared from nowhere, moving simultaneously to the music in full dress, wearing a belt made of coins that was gently placed on her hips as she swirled around the carpet in tune with the musicians. I was mesmerised by her movements. She gracefully left the scene and not expecting any further entertainment as nothing appeared to happen for a while, we stayed on to enjoy the classical music that we were becoming familiar with.

Then quite suddenly, another dancer appeared, showing off an exquisite hipster belt decorated in a mixture of coins, matched by a magnificent sequinned bra which carefully covered her modesty. She floated through the air wearing a flimsy ice-blue chiffon skirt that flowed after her as the ripples of her body magically coincided with the notes of the music. I was in awe.

Watching her, completely hypnotised with her movements, I saw that she was gradually making her way towards our table and, not understanding why she was coming in my direction, I realised as she got hold of my hand that she wanted me to join her. I had no idea what she was going to do with me and had no alternative but to follow her, especially after hearing the hoots and claps from the audience, administering their approval that she had chosen someone. I was completely confused as to what was going to happen next and nervous at the same time. She guided me towards the stage where she encouraged me to copy her gentle movements of the hip, swaying backwards and forwards, which seemed impossible for me to co-ordinate. I tried the best I could, which caused glee in the musicians' eyes as they watched the spectacle. It was a poor attempt, but the dancer continued to show me other movements, which again I tried with difficulty to mimic, much to the amusement of the waiters – trying to hide their cheeky grins – who had probably guessed there would be a victim before the night descended.

The audience joined in clapping and laughing, sounding as though they were enjoying the display, and I accepted the difficulties of the movements the best way I could. Realising my ordeal was finally over, she politely guided me back to the table where Colin was waiting for me, beaming a mighty smile and clapping enthusiastically, together with the warm response from the audience, which I was grateful for.

"Not like me to make an exhibition of myself," I whispered in Colin's ear. He just carried on laughing, showing all his teeth, enjoying the moment and not listening to my excuses. When I felt everything had quietened down, I slowly took the courage to glance back at the dancer and on doing so, I suddenly felt an overwhelming sense of déjà vu that swept over me. It only lasted a split second or two but was powerful enough to make me believe, against all the odds, that I could possibly be in the very same position as that dancer one day.

★

Colin and I returned to London and it was not long before the dreariness of the office took its toll, with the usual heavy, strict routine and monotonous workload.

It was on one Monday morning, whilst coming up from Chancery Lane tube station, that I was handed a free magazine being given out to passers-by as they left the station called *Ms. London*. I did not always bother reading it as I was usually too busy and didn't have the time, but that lunchtime I had a moment to flick through the pages. As I did, my eye caught a tiny advert tucked away in the corner of a page, offering 'Belly Dancing classes, down Southampton Row', just off from where I was working in Holborn. My interest was immediately aroused, and I took the courage to phone the number given in the advert. Before I knew where I was, I had booked myself in for the lessons.

The classes were pay as you go, which meant one could leave the class at any time, allowing students not to be tied down to a course and giving a sense of freedom if it was something that did not suit them. I had no idea what to expect but I was fascinated enough to give it all a go.

The dancing teacher was named Selwa, from the Yemen, a professional dancer in her own right. She had a certain strictness about her, an austere and stern approach that was integral to her nature, and she demanded respect and expected nothing less back from her students in return. There was a certain discipline to the lessons and we all felt it a duty to adhere to her rule. Laughter was minimal. Training had to be taken seriously, with a dedication to reach the heights she had in mind for us.

There were about thirty ladies in the group of all different sizes, shapes, ages and religions, semi-clad in homemade gear, who seemed to not have a care in the world about how they looked or what they wore to the class – which appeared a mish-mash of brightly coloured scarves. It appeared that some just wanted to be skilled enough in the dance to show their Middle Eastern boyfriends or husbands how authentic they could be, whereas others, like myself, went along out of pure interest, curiosity and fun, only to find out that the experience was to be a rude awakening.

The first twenty minutes of the class were made up of exercises that one had not considered possible in a usual exercise class, mainly consisting of bending and stretching, with a similarity to a yoga class. It was important to learn how to separate the top half of one's body from the bottom half, one of the main elements of the dance, and the exercises were intended to help in that capacity.

It took a lot of practice and time to get the body adjusted to some of the movements. Right arm up and left hip drop. Lift left hip but let it drop. Now the other side. One of the difficulties was administering the movements to music that one did not know as Selwa had grown up with the melodies all her life and was able to interpret them in her dance like the back of her hand, whereas, we did not have a clue what was coming next to be ready with a movement.

I found having to dance individually in front of one's classmates, quite nerve-racking at times as they could be quite ruthless and cruel in their judgment without realising it, but worst of all was being scrutinised by Selwa herself, who had a sharp eye for divergence and slip-ups. It was inevitable that we would make mistakes with the choreography of the movements to the music, but it was whether we had the nerve to take the medicine and carry on.

The veil was an added implement where we had to co-ordinate it's movement, with the swaying and circling of it around the body in different directions, whilst at the same time synchronising the hips with the beat of the music. But after a lot of practice and patience, I eventually managed to master how the veil flowed, depending on the material, to coincide with the bodily movements of the dance and after a while felt reasonably comfortable with it.

Finger cymbals were optional but had to be played in a rhythm like the sound of a galloping horse, clickety click, clockety clock, hitting the beat of the music, whilst again remembering to co-ordinate the movements of the body with the harmony of the notes. This was not easy at first, but after much practice, playing the cymbals can become second nature and a useful tool to use as an opening before making an entrance onto the stage.

★

I had been at the classes once a week for about a year when my office colleague Wendy was intrigued to know how I was getting on. She was organising a party at her maisonette in Notting Hill Gate and asked me if I would be interested in doing a show for her guests. I laughed out aloud at the concept, doubting my abilities, and told her I did not think it would be a good idea, and that I was still very much a novice and not up to standard. Not listening to my foreboding, she insisted that it would be a great idea, explaining it would be fun whatever level I had achieved, and that it could be a wonderful party piece at her gathering. I tried again to shy away from it, changing the subject, but she did not give up; she persisted saying it would be a good idea. In the end, I caved in and finally agreed to accept her challenge.

At every spare moment I practised the dance at home to a piece of music from Farid El-Atrache that I felt comfortable with, using the few movements already learnt by keeping it simple, easily alternating them to change in a hypnotic way as the music merged into different stages of the rhythm.

I arrived at Wendy's maisonette early having offered to help her prepare nibbles before everyone arrived for the party, but my mind was constantly drawn to the moment she would ask me to get ready. I wondered if I would still have the nerve to do it when the time came or whether I could change my mind at the last minute, or if she might even forget as the night wore on.

I helped her butter the bread for cucumber sandwiches, attached baby chipolatas, cheese and pineapple chunks to cocktail sticks, and spent time neatly slicing apples and oranges onto plates that were surrounded by strawberries and grapes in a decorative way. Crisps and peanuts were placed in bowls around the flat for those who needed titbits with their drinks, and jacket potatoes were being heated ready for the guests as they arrived, to be served with a sprinkle of cheese on top. It was all quick and easy, not what you would get at the Ritz, but a tasty collection of morsels to satisfy most taste buds, not forgetting plenty of wine and beer to suit everyone's thirst.

Slowly, the guests arrived, bringing their contributions of food and drink to augment what we already had. The music played – mainly songs by familiar pop bands known to us – and the party began.

As the evening moved on, with the wine continuously being poured into empty glasses, small gatherings of people accumulated, getting to know one another and with the food slowly disappearing, the moment finally arrived when Wendy approached me. "I'll take you upstairs, Liz, and show you where you can change and get ready."

I brought a homemade costume that was very basic, consisting of a longish colourful skirt, which I pulled down onto my hips and kept up with various scarves tied around the belt, a tarted-up bra covered in silver coins and wore a bright red band around my head. It was all I had as I did not have a proper costume to wear, but I hoped it would suffice for the event.

Chris Michael, the articled clerk from the office, offered his help by announcing me before placing the Arabic record I had brought along on the gramophone, and Wendy arranged everyone to sit in a circle around the room.

After a while, Chris came running up the stairs to ask if I

was ready, saying he was going to put the music on. I nodded, acknowledging I was, and like a lamb to the slaughter, realising there was no going back, I ventured down the staircase for my cue. The lights were dimmed, and I waited at the bottom of the stairs while Chris announced me. Then I could hear the beginning stages of my music, which prompted me to start playing my finger cymbals to the beat, and I slowly entered the circle of people who had been patiently waiting for my entrance. I tried to thoroughly focus on the choreography I had practised at home over the past few weeks by cutting my mind off from their presence and imagining I was at home practising in front of a mirror.

The atmosphere was intense and to my relief, after the first few minutes of appearing on the stage, the guests showed their appreciation by suddenly cheering and clapping, which was a lovely surprise. Hearing them urge me on helped my anxiety to settle into the music as I began to trust that the partygoers were enjoying the movements, giving me the confidence to carry on. It was all so welcoming and, where there was an area in the music to consider approaching someone to dance with me for fun, I took the courage to venture towards Wendy as she was the host of the party, and to my surprise she happily accepted being my first victim. She went down well, with the audience enjoying her moment, clapping and encouraging her until I eventually guided her back to the circle to choose someone else, but a couple of men came to join me, showing off their abilities, which created hoots of laughter, with others joining in. There was a lot of fun and when the record ended, I managed to finish with a shimmer and a short spin before I was able to run up the stairs to the sanctum of Wendy's bedroom, hearing a rapturous applause behind me, where I took a breather and began to take in what I had just done.

Wendy followed me into the bedroom excitedly saying how everyone had loved the show, words that affected me greatly as it was my first public appearance. Her remarks gave me a sense of confidence that I had not particularly experienced at the classes, and I believe that was the moment the seed had been sewn for what was to come.

★

Whilst at my secretarial post in Holborn and working for Fern Pringle, one of the partners, she informed me that the barrister who would be acting for her in the case she had given me to type was my brother! I was flabbergasted as it was such a coincidence and later that day, the clerk from Jeremy's Chambers called to ask how far I had got on with the typing of the brief as Jeremy was expecting papers to arrive in Chambers that afternoon. When I told him that I was Jeremy's sister and not to worry as I would make sure he would receive the brief by the end of the day, the clerk laughed heartily, saying he would pass on the message, and I typed like the clappers to get it done for him on time. When it was finished and signed by Fern, I tied red ribbon neatly around the papers, showing 'Brief to Counsel' with Jeremy's full name in bold typeset on the front, and Chris Michael kindly delivered it personally to his Chambers in Hare Court without further delay.

A couple of days later, I asked Fern how the case went. "Much better than expected," she said, which sounded like a good result.

★

Gregory Rowcliffe & Co. was one of the happier places I had worked, with a very friendly set of solicitors and staff, but after five years I felt it was time for a change. What that change was going to be, I had no idea at the time as I had nothing planned, but took the brave decision in handing in my notice.

It was usually common practice for the solicitors and secretaries in the firm to give a member of staff a good 'send-off', and Chris Michael, being a close colleague, took the initiative of collecting everyone's contributions towards a gift, which would be presented to me on my last day. Often the person who was leaving dreaded the occasion, preferring to just creep away and disappear, but if one had been there a fair length of time and was retiring or leaving for other reasons, the firm expected them to attend so that everyone could wish them well for the future.

A month's notice is not easy when one has made one's mind up to leave. It drags on. One morning, Chris Michael came into my room all excited, saying he thought it would be a great idea if I could do a show of the dance at my presentation. I laughed at the prospect but he insisted, and we discussed the possibility at great length as to whether it would be appropriate or not as I did not feel confident enough to perform in front of all my work colleagues. He spent some time reassuring me that as he had seen me dance at Wendy's party, I had nothing to worry about, and that it would be a great way to say goodbye.

When the last day of my notice finally arrived, I took my homemade costume to the office with all the other bits and pieces needed for the show, and Chris Michael kindly brought his tape recorder along to help with the music side of things. My heart was thumping all day as I looked at the clock, and later in the afternoon Chris had organised everyone – around fifty people who worked in the firm – to accumulate in one of the larger committee rooms, ready for the presentation. I was as nervous as a kitten. I had danced in front of the girls in the class, which I always found daunting, but nothing prepared me for what I was about to do in front of people I had been working for over the last five years, and it was not as though it would be a party atmosphere where everyone had mingled beforehand. A small buffet of sandwiches and cakes had been placed on tables, with a few bottles of wine for those who fancied a drink, but the atmosphere was tense and hesitant to say the least. Perhaps they felt it could be an embarrassment on my part and uncomfortable for them to watch as they knew I was not a professional, having just danced at the classes, or they might wonder if it could end up as a humiliation, with not knowing what to say afterwards. It was all a complete gamble.

Mary, the receptionist and an ex-police officer, befriended me by acting as my bodyguard whilst changing in the ladies', and Wendy kindly brought me a glass of wine to calm my nerves. It took me a while to change. Chris called out to Mary, stationed at the door, that he was going to put the music on and I ventured down the corridor with Mary at my side as Chris frantically beckoned for me to wait outside the committee room so that he could announce my entrance before starting the tape.

When I heard my music begin I started to play my finger cymbals and entered the room full of solicitors and secretarial colleagues, who were looking at me in disbelief and querying whether I was the person they thought I was. It was a strange moment because I felt as they did, but I said to myself, *I'm here now, I can't hide any more. This is my other half, take it or leave it.* I had not gone into the dance for too long before the senior partner, Mr Hobbs, enthusiastically began to remove his jacket and ventured towards me. Everyone was laughing uncontrollably as he carried out some of the most awkward contortionist movements of the dance I had ever seen, which became the ice-breaking moment. I put my veil around his hips, which did not help his strange contribution, but I played my cymbals most of the time, keeping my equilibrium and dancing around him in the best way I could. Once Mr Hobbs returned to his place, he had paved the way for others to bravely show what they could do by coming out and joining me. Everyone was enjoying the fiasco, clapping and cheering me, with no sign of shyness or embarrassment from any of them, as first thought. When the music ended, after my spin and small bow, I ran down the corridor into the ladies' and looked at myself in the mirror, thinking, "How did I do that?!"

It was a wonderful atmosphere and rather than the daunting occasion I was dreading, it turned out to be quite the opposite.

Whilst changing in the ladies', I heard a woman's high-heeled shoes hurriedly clicking along the corridor, and as she entered the ladies' with a wide smile on her face, still holding her glass of wine, she unexpectedly put her arms around me. "You were marvellous," she said, hugging me, "and you so look the part." It was Fern, who I had been working for over the past five years and her words of genuine encouragement remained with me throughout the rest of my career.

After I changed, I returned to the committee room for the presentation and was stunned to find everyone had contributed towards a new record player as a leaving gift, which Chris Michael believed I would benefit from the most. Then a large card was handed to me with all their signatures, quips and messages written inside, wishing me well for the future. I was so delighted, touched and moved by the warmth and goodwill from everyone at Gregory Rowcliffe & Co., and I prayed I was doing the right thing.

★

It felt strange on Monday morning not returning to my old job, carrying on with the same old familiar routine that I was used to and I even queried whether I might have made a big mistake by leaving. But on the other hand, I knew I had to get away from feeling cocooned in an office atmosphere; I needed space to breathe, and even though I had no idea what I was going to do with nothing organised, I felt it was like starting a fresh page, with the rest of my life ahead of me.

But we all need money to live on, and as my skills were with the secretarial profession I decided to return to temping, where at least I could have more freedom than being permanent in one place. Computers, though, were taking over from typewriters, making it more difficult to jump from one job to another and as firms had their own unique management package they arranged induction courses for the temp to learn their methods before starting work.

I kept a notepad of everything I learnt in each firm as it was expected that I should automatically remember their system if they wanted me back. I also included colleagues' names to save embarrassment if I had forgotten who they were on my return.

The agencies were making good revenue by replacing permanent secretaries, who might suddenly need time off, by sending out temporary staff to solicitors who urgently needed their help. Invariably, the agencies were their lifeline on many occasions.

A lot of temp secretaries needed a job first thing on Monday morning, preferring to wait in the agency in the hope of a week's booking, whilst others found it more suitable to stay at home and wait for the jobs as they came in at all different times of the day. Either way suited the agency as they needed recruits of all sorts to fill whatever positions became available in their books.

There was always a lot of work around for an experienced legal secretary, with good rates of pay by the hour, especially when working through lunch or doing overtime, which not only benefitted the agency, giving them additional revenue, but also the solicitor, who appreciated the extra time given to his workload. It also benefitted the permanent staff who wanted to get away on time at the end of the day.

As I had experience and knowledge of a mixed bag of the law, attained through my working life, I was able to take on most of the opportunities that came in and was never out of work. The positions I used to avoid – or sometimes reject – were Residential and Commercial Conveyancing posts, because their workload generally consisted of typing long leases and filling in endless forms. Typewriters could not save work and if a mistake was made, one had to start the document all over again. It was only when the computer WordPerfect came in that such documents could be changed more easily and kept on the system, but until then they had to be individually, manually typed.

Staff from the conveyancing departments were often off sick because of the stress of the job, which meant temps were frequently needed to fill those vacancies at a moment's notice. I always preferred Litigation or Trust and Probate, where there could be some interesting cases to help the time pass by, but generally the job amounted to typing voluminous documents without much reprieve throughout the day.

★

I joined an agency, Cavendish Personnel – just behind John Lewis in Cavendish Square, London – as they were paying a good rate and specialised in legal vacancies.

Whilst I was being interviewed, I was expected to do a typing and spelling test to prove that I could set out a legal document correctly and show that I had experience and knowledge of the law.

"This is a good CV," said Ingrid, the owner of the agency, as she lifted her head with a beady eye, simultaneously with her assistant Maureen, who smiled in my direction.

"You have worked in barristers' chambers, I see, and have covered most areas of the law, which is very useful. I notice your hobbies are unusual… What's this? Belly dancing!" she said, almost laughing.

"Oh yes," I replied. "It's only a hobby and I go to the classes."
She looked at me and smiled.

"We are having our Christmas party very soon, with a small buffet and wine for the girls. Would you do a show for us?"

I was taken aback for a moment and explained that I was still training at the classes and not professional enough to dance in public, but Ingrid carried on showing personal interest in the hope that I would accept her offer and agree.

"Look," she said bluntly, "I can get you a six-week booking for solicitors with Jay Benning & Co. in Portland Place, which is just down the road from us and on the day of the party I can arrange extra time for lunch, fully paid. What do you say?"

It sounded an offer too good to refuse. When I looked at her, I knew she meant what she was saying and, not wanting to miss a great opportunity, I accepted.

"Excellent," she said and took me over to a desk where I could sign the contract of employment.

I was thrilled. Not only had I been given a six-week secretarial booking, tiding me over for Christmas, but also the chance of dancing in another show, and all without proving I was able to do either! A risk on their part, I thought, but on the other hand, I could not let the opportunity go.

*

The senior partner at the firm of solicitors in Portland Place happened to be a woman, a rarity indeed as there were hardly any women lawyers or barristers – or police, for that matter – in the late 1980s and early 1990s, as they were mainly male-orientated professions. In fact, the agency would ask temps if they minded working for a woman before they sent them out and it would not go against them if they refused. In this case, I was working for the senior partner's husband, a solicitor specialising in litigation. A tall, gentle man, very much under his wife's thumb, he proved to be the easier option to work for out of the two!

I had not told anyone at work about what I had been asked to do at the Christmas party as I did not particularly want to be in the spotlight, and hoped it could all be kept as quiet as possible. The staff at work knew it was the agency's Christmas buffet that day and accepted I would be having a longer lunch than usual with the understanding that it would be limited to temporary secretaries only and was not something they had been invited to, so I felt reasonably safe to a certain extent.

On the day of the party, I was feeling quite apprehensive hearing the other secretaries around me tapping away on their typewriters, completely oblivious to my nerves as I anxiously watched the minutes tick away on the big clock on the wall. The fluorescent lights shone from the ceiling, demanding their supremacy, as I kept my secret hidden, touching the travel bag at my feet every now and again in reassurance that it was still there and to remind me that I had not forgotten anything: my costume, the tape recorder (as I had promised to supply the music), the tape, jewellery, perfume, veil, finger cymbals; everything I needed to help create the fantasy of what I was trying to project for a crowd of secretaries I had never met before.

By the time I had arrived at the agency, the party was already well under way and Ingrid hustled me into the back room, where the coats of all the girls were lying around. "Would you like a glass of wine?" she said, trying to put me at ease. It was the best thing I had heard all day and I began to prepare myself for what was to come. I put plenty of glistening bangles on my wrists and tied different coloured scarves in knots around my hips to accentuate the movements, which I hoped would add an extra element to the dance.

The next thing I knew, I could hear my music starting and Ingrid opened the door. I began to play my finger cymbals to the rhythm of the music as I entered the arena of girls, all standing around balancing plates and glasses in both their hands. Then, to my amazement, in the corner of my eye I spotted the litigation solicitor I had been working for in Portland Place standing amongst the throng of women encircled around the room. He turned out to be my saviour because when I glided over to him, he happily followed me into the centre of the room, where I showed him how to portray some of my movements. It was all so funny. He really did try his best. Dignity was pushed aside as he pranced around in his pin-striped suit, not knowing how to react. I wrapped the veil around his thin waist to help him get a feel of the dance and there were shrieks of laughter as I tied the flimsy material around him. The girls loved it as he helplessly moved around in a circle with his thin hips slanting in all directions, and clapped him on, wanting more fun. He was a good sport and got a good applause. I managed to bring a few of the girls out to have a go before I finished with a shimmer and small spin that I had rehearsed to end the show, when I noticed staff workers from the offices across the road waving from the windows with signs of thumbs up as I ran back into the changing room, hearing cheers of applause from the girls behind me. I knew it had been a success.

Ingrid asked me to stay behind afterwards as she wanted to talk to me, and after I had changed, I sat at the desk opposite her waiting for her to finish her call. Then, she gave me a Christmas present of a box of chocolates and two bottles of white wine, thanking me for the show as an added gift, which was a lovely suprise.

"Stay there a minute," she said as she hurriedly wrote down

the telephone number of a restaurant she knew in Hendon owned by a Turkish Cypriot, Ata Chalayan, who did little shows himself to please the customers as she believed he might be interested in having a belly dancer as an added element of entertainment. I was blown away by her gesture as it meant she thought I looked professional enough to dance in public at a restaurant, which could take my hobby to a more serious level. She smiled as she passed me his number insisting that I give Ata a ring.

I kept his number in my purse for months before I could gain the courage to call him.

*

Christmas had come and gone, and I had left my temp position in Portland Place. The telephone number Ingrid had given me was getting grubby and tearing around the edges in my purse, looking like a lost, forgotten bus ticket. I could not find the courage to work in a restaurant with real customers as I had a certain naivety about dancing in public, especially with my limited experience of having just practised with the girls in class.

My concerns were what the customers would think of me, whether they would make fun of me and not take me seriously; that the owner would ridicule me, knowing the dance better than I did; that I might find myself in danger, particularly working at night with the hazards that night work could bring; and that my dreams might disintegrate overnight, like the shabby piece of paper in my purse. It was a big decision to make and every time I tried to muster the courage to pick up the phone to speak to Ata, I immediately put it down again, thinking better of it.

The other difficulty I had was informing my teacher, Selwa, at the dancing class, as she warned us quite openly at the beginning of each class that she would bar any girl who was found to be working as a belly dancer in restaurants and clubs from being able to return to her class for further tuition ever again.

She called her dance 'Raks Shaki', which is a more modern version of the belly dance, and her movements were classical like a ballet dancer, yet had a folk element contained in the story. She was a professional dancer, attracting audiences from not only the Middle East but from all over the world to watch her on the stage. She knew the music back to front, having been brought up with the traditional sounds from childhood and having mastered how to choreograph her style to perfection.

In Selwa's world – or generally in the Arab world, it seemed – the belly dance was associated with prostitution, and unmarried girls or women would dance in the markets and town centres in the hope that the public would throw coins to show their appreciation. The money was thrown near their feet or collected into basket-type containers and the coins were later sewn into their hip scarves, worn around their waist as an attachment to their costumes to show off their wares.

The belly dance was also a form of public entertainment where traveller tribes from both Egypt and Turkey would perform in the streets. In Egypt, the ethnic group was called ghawazi. They would dance outdoors and in front of coffee houses during public processions. The tribe would sing and dance, using props such as canes and swords to add to their repertoire. In the 1920s the nightclubs flourished, and the dance was performed for audiences made up mainly of Europeans, which caused the dance style to change to please a foreign audience. This is where Raks Shaki was born, a spin-off from the belly dance. One of the most famous nightclubs in Cairo in that era belonged to Badiia Masabni, and this was where the dance was adapted for the stage to a set choreography and performances were introduced. The costumes changed – up until that point, dancers wore a wide long skirt, a shirt and a waistcoat, but from the 1920s, dancers started wearing what is known today as a typical belly dancer's costume (bedlah) consisting of a bra, a skirt, a bare midriff, veils and a lot of glitter and beads and the Egyptian dancers wore body stockings to cover their bare flesh.

I had been in Selwa's class for over a year, watching her in awe as we saw her dance not only on the stage at performances, but also in front of us, where we hoped we could achieve a good enough level to please her, but we all knew we could never accomplish the same heights that she had reached.

Westerners usually call the dance the 'belly dance' and even though I lacked a certain confidence to dance in public, I was drawn to the fact that my experience would not end with just attending the classes. I felt I was being drawn into a karmic role and had a strong sense that Fate would play a part in that journey, asking me to follow the guidelines, signs and opportunities that were offered to me. I already found it strange that my first important opening to becoming an entertainer was through an unlikely source, such as a temping secretarial agency and was beginning to understand that if I had remained at Gregory Rowcliffe, the opportunity would never have presented itself in the same way.

One thing that was pulling me back was my conscience. I felt a certain sense of guilt knowing that Selwa would be against my taking the dance any further, causing me to reconsider my intentions of working outside the classes until I finally decided to confront her by writing her a letter explaining what I was planning to do. I expressed my gratitude for how much I had enjoyed her classes over the year, but said that I wanted to pursue the dance further in restaurants – and eventually in clubs when I had more experience – and that I hoped she would accept my attendance in future if I could reassure her that I would never discuss my dancing pursuits with the other students. In the meantime, I would like to leave her a little gift and enclosed a cheque with my thanks. I did not know how she was going to react, but felt better for being honest.

When I arrived at the class a day or two later, Selwa immediately came over to thank me for the letter and the gift, telling me to carry on in her class if I kept to my word by not discussing my new activities with anyone else. I was so pleased she had taken that stance as I had close friends there – Joannie, Helen and Sheila from Mauritius – who were hoping I could stay on, and when they understood I was to remain in the class, they were sworn to secrecy about what I was to do.

But for me, the green light had been shown and the next step was whether I had the courage to consider giving Ata a ring.

★

The agencies always had several solicitors on their books that were often blacklisted by the temps, who would never return to a job that they were unhappy in, and the agency was always advertising for new recruits to fill those roles. The only way blacklisted firms could fill their vacancies was to pay a higher hourly rate, which sadly did not always get handed down to the temp, but the agency would always look after the temps who accepted some of the more difficult and challenging jobs by keeping them in work throughout the year.

The best time to temp was during the summer months, when permanent secretaries were on holiday, offering a different selection of firms from those who used temps all year round. Sometimes I would get sent out to firms that I had often wondered whether I would like to work for them or not and when I got there, realised they were not at all as I had imagined. On other occasions whilst working in a firm of solicitors, I would recognise my initials on a letter sent from the firm I had worked for the week before, and when that happened I openly boasted to my colleagues in the office how nicely typed the letter was, which usually caused a lot of sarcastic laughter from everyone.

Permanent staff, who preferred the security and stability of a job, frequently asked me questions about where I had been and what I felt about some of the places I had worked in and I was more than happy to share some of my experiences with them, especially if they were going for an interview or were thinking of applying for a new job.

But the best way to survive as a temp was to be friendly, adaptable and to work things out for oneself rather than annoying the surrounding staff by constantly needing their assistance, to get the workload done, remember names and offer to make tea.

★

Ingrid got me another booking at Doolittle & Dalley Solicitors near Holborn, and the moment I entered reception, I was hit straight away by the feeling of doom and gloom that was beginning to feel familiar with in so many of the office atmospheres.

"I'll get someone to show you where to go," said the disinterested receptionist. "Anna will be down in a minute." I waited in reception listening to the phone ring, clients arriving for their appointments and the post being delivered, when a stout lady appeared in front of me with shoulder-length hair and wearing well-pronounced rimmed glasses, saying my name with a slight smile. "Elizabeth Gordon? I'm Anna. This way, please."

We squashed ourselves into a tiny lift that creaked and swayed as it slowly elevated upwards. "You will be working for a Mr Sly in Commercial Conveyancing. Did you come far?" There was the usual banter till the lift came to an abrupt stop and we both tried to open the heavy iron gates. "This way," she said as we started walking down the long corridor.

The bland, chestnut brown carpet reminded me of timelessness and as I walked along the passageway, I felt a tingle of static electricity underfoot. We passed rooms to the left and the right, some with their doors tightly shut and others ajar or open, where I could see solicitors at work, studying their papers with complete disinterest in who was passing by. We had walked a fair way down the corridor when Anna made an abrupt stop to lightly tap on one of the doors, where we quietly waited. "Enter," we heard in a shrill voice from behind the closed door.

A small, balding man sat behind a large desk by the window, looking over his half-moon glasses that were nearly falling off the end of his nose. "This is Elizabeth. She has come to work for you," Anna told him. He glanced over his spectacles as he scrutinised me with his cold, sharp blue eyes. "Have you done any commercial conveyancing?" he asked in a shallow voice. I could see he lacked sensitivity, empathy and humour, and had a complete disinterest in my personal wellbeing; all he was concerned about was how fast I could type, how accurate my work would be and how resilient I could be to cope with his heavy workload. I was fully aware that the agency had already informed him of my capabilities, thus my reason for being there, so I did not feel it was necessary on his part to patronise me in such a way. He looked at me with a pugnacious expression on his face and a wry smile gave the impression that the introduction had taken place, he had nothing further to say and, as he was a busy man, it was time for me to leave. I almost felt it was my duty to bow and walk backwards towards the door, but my rebellious sense of humour thought better of it and accepted that the only respite I was going to get was by removing myself from the room as soon as I could, without a hiccup.

Further down the corridor, Anna opened another door to a bevy of secretaries busily working on their typewriters, not even lifting their heads to see who had entered the room. They were under pressure and had no time to be curious. The office was filled with papers, books and masses of old files, with a smell of dust in the air. The heavy sound of typewriters pounded all around me and I suddenly felt an overwhelming sense of claustrophobia.

Anna stopped the tension by saying, "This will be your desk," showing me a tiny table in the corner of the room facing a blank wall. "All the forms for conveyancing are in those drawers over there, and these two full tapes on the top of these files are very urgent, while this pile here is half-finished by the previous secretary, which I suggest you start first". I imagined that there had been many secretaries who had been sitting at the desk working for Mr Sly and I observed that my predecessor must have walked out of the job, thus the reason for a tape being left half-finished. "Also," she said, "Mr Sly has some urgent bits and pieces he needs doing today – alright?"

"Yes, thank you," I said politely as I watched her leave the room. It was too late to run.

The first thing was to familiarise myself with the IBM Golfball, as electric typewriters were still very popular. It hummed as I switched it on. A strange keyboard always takes a while to get adjusted to for touch-typing, but once I had orientated myself with the layout, I found it was easy enough to get acquainted. The Grundig tape recorder was similar to what I had used before, but the earplugs felt tatty and well-used, as the HR department hadn't replaced them with new ones before my arrival. The foot pedal squeaked, needing oiling, but not wanting to cause trouble or waste more time, I decided to put my head down to accustom myself with the equipment and Mr Sly's dreary, dull and monotonous dictation for the rest of the day.

Later in the week, I phoned the agency to get me another job. Ingrid replied in the same way they do when they need you to stay on at a booking they have organised for you. "I have not got anything else in at present. If you could just hang on until the end of the week, I will try and get you something for next week."

I got through the week but on Friday morning I got a call from Ingrid. "Liz, they want you back next week. I haven't been able to get anything else for you, it is quiet at the moment, please stay another week." It was the same old story but I insisted I was only going to do one more week, which I hoped she would understand.

On Friday evening I met some of my friends from the dancing class, Joannie and Helen, for a drink after work and we went to our favourite wine bar, Gordons, down Villiers Street near the Embankment, one of the oldest drinking holes in London, erected in the thirteenth century. It did not need a licence to trade and looked like a shop outside, with an old brown door hiding its entrance. We shared a bottle of wine together and my friends laughed uncontrollably as I mocked and made fun of Mr. Sly to my heart's content. I had heard his voice in my ears all week which enabled me to mimic him exceptionally well and I said - 'Have you ever done any Conveyancing in your life, as I know far more than you?' and 'Leave the room, I'm far too busy, I don't want to be distracted by the likes of you.' I managed to get my friends rolling over with laughter at the very mention of Mr Sly, who would have been distraught at my open humour if he had overheard me, and thoroughly shocked at the way I portrayed him, when he possibly imagined he was well looked up to.

On my way home that night, I passed an empty telephone box. *I have nothing to lose,* I said to myself. Feeling brave and in a good mood I shuffled around for the piece of paper with the telephone number of the Chalayan restaurant that was somewhere in my purse. It was still there, with plenty of coins to make the call. My heart thumped as I dialled the number. It kept ringing and I waited. Eventually, a man answered.

"Hello."

"Hello, is that Ata Chalayan?"

"Yes," he replied. He sounded abrupt at first, but I carried on.

"A lady called Ingrid said she knows you and thought you might need a belly dancer."

"Who?" he said.

"Ingrid," I repeated, but by now I felt he could not recall her.

"What is your name?" he asked.

"Elizabeth."

"Where are you?" he asked.

"I'm in Highgate, I'm on my way home. I would just like to say that I did a show for the secretarial agency and Ingrid gave me your number."

"You come tomorrow, bring your costume and you do audition. Ring me from Hendon Central station around 8pm. I will collect you by car. OK?"

I put the phone down. I had done it!

★

The next day I decided to use the same piece of music, Hizzi Ya Nawaim played by George Abdo and his orchestra, which I had chosen for the agency's Christmas party. It was an exhilarating piece with plenty of drums crashing around to help accentuate hip movements, with a shortened version of the taksim portraying the slower part of the dance before finishing with a short spin. The tape was approximately twenty minutes long, edited to remove lengthy adagio areas from the music in order to keep the attention of an audience in a restaurant. I played the tape all day long so I could feel comfortable enough to ad lib if necessary and spent time sewing coins and other bits and bobs I had bought from the bead shop in Covent Garden to my homemade costume, and carefully threaded silver beading through my head band to make it sparkle. The costume jewellery was polished to shine and glitter as it needed care, not being expensive stuff, and I made sure my finger cymbals could fit safely on the end of my fingers without easily falling off. I practised the dance at every available moment so that I could feel at ease with my own choreograph, knowing Selwa would not be there to guide me. This was something I had to do on my own.

The night eventually drew in, getting dark, and just when everyone else was settling down for a cosy night in, I was getting ready to brave the night air with the feeling that I was about to experience a completely strange new world that could make me feel vulnerable in my naivety.

I arrived at Hendon Central tube and made a call to the restaurant from a phone box in the station, as was agreed the night before. Ata answered straight away. "Hello," he said in a booming voice.

"Ata, it's Elizabeth, I am at the station."

"OK," he replied. "Wait there, I come to collect you."

I nervously waited outside the station in the dark for a strange man who was going to collect me in an unknown car and take me to a destination I had only heard about. People looked at me, wondering if I was loitering or had a purpose there, and I gave some of them a double take, wondering if they were Ata as I had no idea what he looked like. Eventually a car pulled up and a rather large man inside leant over to open the passenger door with a big smile on his face. He did not get out of the car but shouted to me, saying that he was Ata. "Get in," he ordered – which I did! All my mother had told me about not getting into strange cars went by the board and, without my asking him where we were going, he put his foot on the accelerator and off we went.

When we arrived at the restaurant, I was immediately impressed by the warm atmosphere awaiting us with the playing of jolly music in the background. Pretty chandeliers twinkled their lights onto the wine bottles all neatly lined up on shelves and decorated the maroon-coloured walls, giving off a sense of affluence and high living. There was a touch of Morocco embedded in the surroundings and I immediately felt at home.

Ata led me through to a small bar area at the end of the restaurant where there was a welcoming man behind the counter, drying glasses. "This is Pepe, he is Spanish," said Ata.

"Hello," he said, showing off his white teeth, beaming a magical smile from ear to ear. Then I was ushered round to a little room opposite the kitchen.

"Leave your coat and bags here and join us, I have some guests who would like to meet you." It was all very pleasant and friendly, not as I had imagined an audition to be.

The restaurant already had a few busy tables that Pepe was looking after but Ata beckoned for me to join him and sit with his six male friends by the window, introducing them to me one by one around the table. He had put on a generous spread of different mezes, passing them round and expecting me to try each one. His guests put olives and pieces of melon on the end of cocktail sticks and placed the food in my mouth, which I could not refuse. I learnt it was a Turkish Cypriot gesture of accepting a new guest as a friend. Every time I sipped my wine, my glass was instantly refilled, which I did not always notice, and the chatter was jovial with a lot of laughter – what about I cannot remember, but I laughed anyway. As the evening moved on, Ata eventually whispered in my ear, "It's time – go and change."

I went into the little room opposite the kitchen and was grateful I had been given plenty of time to change as it gave me an opportunity to settle my nerves. Eventually, Ata opened the door, asking me if I was ready. He was a big man – there was not a lot of room for both of us – but he brushed passed me to put my tape in the music centre. Pepe opened the door. "Ooh la la," he said, his black eyes shining. Ata passed him a drum to play and placed a fez on his head to look the part. I was sensing it was serious business and Ata began to announce me over the tannoy. "Hello, ladies and gentlemen. We have a young lady all the way from Egypt who is going to dance for us tonight, her name is…" I did not have a dancing name! There was dead silence, until he came up with 'Shariffa', which I was told meant 'cheers' – 'Serefe' in Turkish – and I liked it.

The music started. Ata put a fez on his head and quickly grabbed a tambourine to play, expecting me to follow, which I did, playing my finger cymbals to the waiting audience. On my entrance, I managed to focus on the choreography I had practised before Ata guided me towards the table where we had been sitting with his group of friends. One of them got up from his seat, insisting I stand on his chair, and before I knew where I was, the others assisted me onto the table. There was no room to manoeuvre amongst the plates of meze, even though the guests hurriedly tried to adjust some of the dishes of hummus, tzatziki, stuffed vine leaves and lentil meatballs, as well as the utensils and wine glasses, to make room for me to move along the tables. It was impossible to show any movements of the dance whilst treading carefully around the plates and I am sure I put my foot on a mushroom or a tomato or something but everyone seemed to be thoroughly enjoying themselves, not caring about the difficulty I was having, which gave me confidence to just carry on. Ata's guests placed tips all around my costume, while customers sitting on the other tables joined in, laughing, clapping and placing tips in my bra and hipster belt. When it was time to finish, I was relieved when one of the guests took my hand to help me down, first onto the chair and then onto dry land as I carried on to finish the show.

I bowed after a small spin, before running back to the dressing room, hearing the applause behind me. Ata followed me, bellowing 'Umpa' as he squeezed himself into the room with me. "Good," he said. "You come next Saturday – OK?"

I was thrilled. I had got myself a lovely little job as a dancer for the weekends and I wanted to shout 'whoopee' – but I did not in public, of course!

★

Ata showed me the ropes and how to work for tips from the customers, helping me feel more confident as the weeks and months went by. I never missed an opportunity to work there and always looked forward to the weekends, when I could be Shariffa.

It was not easy at first, letting go of Elizabeth – the lady who had been working all day in an office, struggling with the hustle and bustle of the London traffic and tackling with the general stresses of life – to suddenly appear as Shariffa, looking as though she had slept all day and spent her waking hours grooming herself and bathing in asses' milk, as did Cleopatra. An illusion difficult to attain, but the atmosphere at the restaurant, with its vibrancy and friendly attitude, always lifted my spirits. Sometimes, to fill time, I would pop into the kitchen to have banter with the staff. Hassan, the chef, being a very funny man, had a knack of making me laugh by showing me strange-shaped vegetables and saying silly things and making up stories about them. Also, I helped Mary with the dishes and dried some of the cutlery for her. They all worked so hard with long hours but there was a sense of camaraderie, everyone getting along well together in idle chatter, and when Hassan treated me to a tub of tzatziki, freshly made that day, to take home with some pitta bread, I felt a million dollars!

Ata was a natural connoisseur in his profession, very charismatic and able to resurrect an empty atmosphere into sheer fun and excitement with just a flick of his fingers. He knew which music to play, changing the tempo at a whim, fully in control of whatever mood he wished to create. Everyone relied on his expertise to entertain them.

Saturday was the busiest night of the week, with all the tables booked to capacity. While I changed in the little dressing room, Ata and Pepe performed their own show, wearing enormous sombreros on their heads and brightly coloured ponchos thrown over their shoulders as they played the castanets to South American music. The female customers waited with baited breath, wondering if they would be the one chosen to dance with them. Even though Ata was a big man, he was light on his feet and a good dancer and liked to show off to the ladies what he could do. As I was preparing to get myself ready, with the atmosphere having already been brought to a crescendo, by the time Ata announced me, all I had to do was just look the part. I never spoke during a performance; I pretended I was an Arabic dancer with the hope that the audience would believe I was genuine. Ata would often place money in my costume as a starter to show customers what was to be done. Whilst he jangled his tambourine to the tempo of the music, with Pepe close by playing the drums, he would guide me to certain customers who he felt would tip me well. Some customers tipped to acknowledge tradition, others did it to please Ata, and there were those who just wanted to join in and show their appreciation with the rest of the crowd.

There was no doubt that he had an aptitude for making his customers feel special, and I also was lured into his magnetic spell, believing that I was special too. He made me feel part of the family and I loved it there.

★

*"Schooners" house built in Seaford*

*My Father with Jeremy on his knee*

*Windmill Down, Rottingdean*
*Standing next to Jeremy (my brother) with Sammy in my arms*

The family at Monte Carlo

The family arriving in Madrid

*In riding gear for boarding school with Sammy at my side*
*On holiday in Alassio, Italy*

*The family in a Kasbah, Tangier, Morocco*

*On 'Baltika', the cruiser ship on its way to Russia*

*(L) His Honour Judge W.E.Monier-Williams touching his wig*
*(R) Tom Sargent OBE (founder of 'Justice')*

*(L) Jeremy Gordon LLB (Hons) Barrister at Law*
*(R) Jeremy's wedding reception. Judy (left)*

Elizabeth Gordon

Elizabeth Gordon

Elizabeth Gordon

*Pen and Ink drawings I sold at Sweet & Maxwell Chancery Lane*

At a staff table in a Turkish club

(L) Jeremy's wedding anniversary
(R) Lunch hour in Covent Garden

*(L) Pepe and Ata at the Chalayan*
*(R) Photo taken by Chris Michael for portfolio*

*(L) Dancing for my audition at the Chalayan*
*(R) Dancing at the Chalayan on a Saturday night*

Colin and I carried on meeting for drinks after work at the end of the week, but he seemed bemused that I had gone to the lengths of getting myself a job dancing at the weekends in public rather than just keeping my enjoyment of the dance to the classes. He thought I was spending far too much time at the restaurant when we could have gone out with one another and he felt we were not meeting up as much as we should. I shared most things with him as we knew each other well, but for some reason I felt I was walking on a tricky tightrope when he asked me personal questions about Ata, such as how often I saw him, what he was like and what I thought of him, etc, etc.

Colin sensed that something was different in my attitude towards him and I found it awkward to explain, other than that my attention was being drawn towards my dancing career with all the energy enthused around it, but I knew he felt it was more than that.

He knew something had changed. We talked well into the night and chatted about our feelings for one another at some length until we came to the realisation that our relationship was not a romantic one. It was difficult as we had been such good friends, getting on so well together, having the same humour, enjoying the same subjects and sharing the same interests – apart from the belly dancing – but I felt that there was that little something missing, that sparkle. Or perhaps it was just the fact that my needs were changing and that my attention was being taken up with other things.

Maybe the dancing was making me feel alive after feeling like I was dying whilst sitting at a desk. Maybe I was becoming more confident within myself, finding my way. Or maybe it was because I had found someone who saw something more in me than just being a secretary.

Life had become exciting.

I was not fully aware of what was changing within me, but

whatever it was, for the time being, Colin accepted that we remain good friends.

★

As the restaurant became very popular with business doing well, customers returning, bringing their friends who brought their friends, not wanting them to tire of me, I realised I needed a lot more costumes.

I did not know how to go about buying them or know where to go, when to my luck and surprise, I saw a small advertisement in a local newspaper by a dancer who was retiring and selling some of her costumes, saying if interested to contact her at a certain PO address. It was a wonderful opportunity not to be missed.

When I arrived at her luxury flat in St John's Wood, I found her to be a very sophisticated but friendly lady who was quite happy to discuss some of her life experiences with me as a professional dancer who had travelled all over the world. I was offered something to eat and drink before she showed me her wardrobe, filled with beautiful dresses and costumes that she had accumulated over the years.

As we went through her repertoire, she picked out three costumes she wanted to sell, explaining that she had originally bought them in Egypt and felt they might suit me. They were exquisite. A beautiful pale blue and silver costume lay in my arms for trying on as she added another one, bright red and gold with the veils to match, and moving along the hangers with a smile, she topped those two with a magnificent turquoise and gold costume to finish. "You can change in the bedroom," she said, leading me into another room. When I tried them on, I was lucky enough to find they fitted perfectly apart from needing a slight adjustment to the hems as she was taller than me. I decided to buy all three without any further thought, which seemed to delight her, not only because of a successful sale but because they had gone to a good home, which appeared important to her.

*

Costumes were very expensive to buy, even second-hand, but as I was finding myself getting fully booked for parties and regularly performing at the Chalayan, I knew I needed more clothes. The question was how, as I did not have the funds to buy such expensive items.

When I looked more closely at the new costumes I had bought, I began to see a little more clearly how they were made. I was fascinated by the intricate work of the delicate stitches, finding that each sequin had been carefully sewn next to one another, and I wondered if it was something I could do myself, although sewing had never been my forte, having often been bottom of the class at school for needlework.

It was an intimidating prospect at first, not knowing where to begin, but I went down to the markets to observe the materials displayed on the stalls and was impressed at what I saw. Fine silks, cloth and fabrics with unusual designs – which I thought would look colourful and spectacular for my purpose – were being sold at a good price, and I bought thousands of beads and sequins from a shop in Covent Garden. I spent hours practising, threading fine cottons through the tiniest of needles and sewing the beads onto fabric, and even though my first attempts did not aspire to much at first, I never gave up and eventually created something that looked reasonable from my handiwork. Everything had to be done by hand as the beading could not be done on a sewing machine and persisted until I achieved the results I was looking for. It was painstaking work. I could never really get the bra exactly like the ones I had bought from the dancer in St John's Wood, but I was able to get a reasonable likeness. I made the belts to my own unique style, with very long strands of beads hanging from the holster belt to accentuate the movements of the dance. Each strand took time and patience, and I was sewing every available moment, accepting it could not be done in a hurry.

After completing the first costume in my favourite colours, black and silver, it gave me hope and inspiration to work on another until I eventually created a collection of costumes, varying in a vast range of vibrant colours and designs, taking many weeks and months.

Music had to be edited from the Arabic records onto cassette tapes for small or large audiences, depending on the venue. With some of the leftover beads I made my own costume jewellery – necklaces, bracelets and head bands in different colours to match the new designs I had made.

I also acquired a few smart cocktail dresses from the fairs and markets to wear for mingling with members of the audience, who sometimes asked me to sit with them and join them at their tables if I had time after the show.

Chris Michael offered to help with a personal portfolio as he had taken up photography as a hobby. I accepted his offer. He owned a flat down Gray's Inn Road, not far from the office, making a perfect opportunity to take advantage of empty rooms whilst vacant and waiting for suitable tenants. We spent an afternoon taking pictures; my posing, pretending to be Shariffa, whilst Chris put on an act imagining he was a film director with an expensive camera. All light-hearted fun. We were free from the office drill. It was a sense of escape in the hope that fantasy might turn into reality as a magical twist.

★

I was beginning to feel more professional and changing into beautiful clothes and costumes made all the difference, as I gradually learnt how to let Elizabeth disappear into the background when I mastered how to allow Shariffa to take over at a whim.

As the weeks and months went by, Ata saw my progress and remarked on my new costumes, saying how spectacular they looked, which gave me the inspiration to create many more in different colours and designs. They took months to complete but were a satisfying pastime in between my secretarial and dancing venues.

"I want you to dance at my house," Ata said. "I have a big party on Sunday."

I arrived at his five-bedroom house in Elstree early Sunday morning as he wanted me to meet the guests as they arrived. The party was to be held in his garden in daylight, not something I was used to after the dim lighting at the restaurant. I prepared myself for what I understood to be a solo performance, limited to the stage only rather than edging around the audience for tips as they were personal guests of his, and one where I would not be accompanied by anyone to help direct my next move. The show was to be created and choreographed entirely on my own with the lawn as my stage in the garden and as I always danced barefoot, I hoped I would not step on a worm or a snail or anything else on the grass that might make me shriek in despair and that if I did, I would keep my nerve and carry on as would be expected of me.

Ata greeted me, opening the door wearing a thick dressing gown, scratching his head and yawning as he directed me to the kitchen, where he slumped down in a chair and buried his head in a newspaper.

"This is my son," Ata said from behind the newspaper and to my surprise, there was a little boy sitting at the other end of the long breakfast table. I knew that Ata was in the process of divorcing his wife, but I was not aware that his son had just left his mother in Cyprus to live with his Father in the UK, and presumed he had just arrived. A sudden shiver of guilt crept over me as I kept my gaze from the boy for a split second or two. My thoughts were confused. I was concerned he would wonder who I was and what connection I had with his Father, especially as I had been invited personally to his home. Had he heard about me? What did he know?

At first, I could not look directly at the boy as I knew what it was like to lose a parent to another and concerned he might think I was taking his father away from his mother. It was a tricky moment. Eventually I took the courage to face the consequences and made eye contact with him.

"Hello, I'm Hussein. What is your name?" he said as he greeted me with an Elvis Presley twist to his lip and a pair of dancing brown eyes. It was a wonderful moment to see him smiling back at me in such a welcoming manner.

"Would you like a cup of coffee? I've just made it," he said.

I nodded and sat down at the table with him as he got another cup and saucer from the cupboard, making me feel at ease.

I had not mixed with too many children in my life and did not know what to expect but I was pleasantly surprised as I found Hussein to be a very intelligent little boy, speaking perfect English as he asked me a bevy of questions about myself, which I tried to answer as accurately as I could. He seemed very self-assured for his 11½ years, like a little adult, and I just knew, the moment I set eyes on him, that he would go far in life. That tricky moment earlier on, not knowing whether I would be accepted by him or not, was well forgotten by the time we started talking to one another and I was touched by the generosity of his nature.

Ata grunted as he got up from his chair, holding his back as though it was causing him pain and saying he was going to have his bath and get ready for his guests, who were going to arrive around midday. Hussein and I smiled after him and continued with our chatter.

We talked about various subjects. He wanted to know all about my travels and where I had been.

I told him all about my trip to Russia, sailing on the cruise ship *Baltika*, landing at Copenhagen and Helsinki before arriving in Leningrad and travelling by overnight train to Moscow. His eyes opened in wonder, encouraging me to tell him more, and I told him as much I could remember about the trip.

We chatted a long while around the breakfast table about all sorts of things as he wanted to know everything that I knew, and I enjoyed sharing what I knew with him, although I never felt it was necessary to tell him anything about my secretarial career, which was like another world, completely forgotten and non-existent.

After a while, we wandered into the garden. It looked lovely. It was such a beautiful summer's day with the sun beating down on the freshly mowed lawn as Hussein recited the names of some of the flowers around us that were unbeknown to me – such long names for a little boy. Along the way he picked a few homegrown strawberries for me to try as we strolled down to the tiny stream at the bottom of the garden, where we stopped to admire the wildlife playing all around us.

Eventually, the guests began to arrive. Most of them came from London but others had come from further afield; a mixed group of people from all over the country. Ata had brought someone in to help with the catering although most of the hard work had already been prepared the night before as he wanted to spend his time organising the barbeque outside on the patio. He was back to his flamboyant self, entertaining the guests and making sure everyone had something on their plates. The wine flowed, music played, and everyone began to mingle. Soon the aroma of spicy food filled the air and plenty of chatter and laughter echoed around the garden as a few angelic children in the most glorious outfits ran around with little offerings of sweets on trays, begging the guests to try one. It was impossible to say no. The dishes of food were endless, and there was an atmosphere of merriment and expectation.

When the party was in full swing, Ata found me in the crowd. "Get ready," he said, and little Hussein came up to me saying he would show me where to go and change. I was led to his bedroom at the back of the house, overlooking the garden, where I could peep through the half-drawn curtains to witness the festivities taking place below.

"I'll come back later," Hussein said excitedly.

I was left a fair while and I could hear the party outside gathering momentum when there was a soft tap on the door. It was Hussein with a glass of dry white wine. Such a welcome thought. He looked in awe at my costume and I put my finger cymbals on and we both laughed as I played them aimlessly to the music outside. Then I could hear his Father in the distance as he was coming up the stairs. He was calling my name. Hussein ran out of the room and Ata entered, saying, "Ready?!"

★

The Chalayan was getting very busy with parties during the week besides the weekends and I would often hope that the secretarial agency would abstain from calling me quite so often with a new job, when Ingrid called to say she had a position that might suit me. I reminded her that I was not looking at legal work as being my main career, whereupon she explained that it was only while the partner's permanent secretary was visiting Australia on a break, and that she did not want to lose the firm's clientele.

I was to be working for the head of the department in

commercial conveyancing at a well-known firm of solicitors, Blythe Dutton in Lincoln's Inn Fields, next to the John Soane Museum that often displays Egyptian artefacts. I was concerned about the position as it was a side of the law I had always tried to avoid. Ingrid expressed that the post was not the usual run of the mill and that they were aware of my other pursuits and would be willing to accept my flexible hours, so in the end, I accepted the position.

The offices were quite modern for the area with spacious open-plan rooms and long windows overlooking Lincoln's Inn Fields. When Mike, head of the department, introduced himself, he greeted me with a firm handshake and a big open smile. There was a gregarious flair about him and I found him easy to get on with as he lay back in his chair in a jovial manner, telling me that he was an ex-rugby player, having changed his life midfield to take up law. I thought it a strange but interesting mixture with a different approach to what I was used to, in that he wanted me to work *with* him rather than *for* him – teamwork in other words, unlike other solicitors' attitudes I had experienced over the years.

He asked me about my dancing career and what nights were difficult. I explained I was always 'on call' at the Chalayan for parties during the week, which would be early evening shows, but that Saturday was the main night at the restaurant.

He told me his days were taken up with meetings in the mornings followed by lengthy lunches which he hoped I could organise by booking tables at some of the most salubrious restaurants and hotels in London as, he said, it was necessary to impress his clients, property developers he was to entertain.

"There are three big files on my hot list," he said proudly. "Crusader House, Little Britain and Canary Wharf" and that after his return from lunch he would need to dictate to me in shorthand for the rest of the afternoon.

He then stood up from his desk, clapping his hands as though the arrangement was already agreed, assuring me that we could amalgamate our hours to suit both of us and that he hoped we could work well together whilst his permanent secretary was away touring Australia - and I told him I was happy to accept.

I started work the next morning and greeted some of his clients as they arrived for their meeting. Well-dressed businessmen, very confident in their manner, enjoying the attention as I escorted them into Mike's office, where we all joined in some quick hearty chatter before I asked them what they would like to drink.

"Get the 4X, Liz," said Mike loudly, whereupon the group acknowledged they liked the order, chuckling in agreement.

There were always plenty of cans of 4X beer stored in the refrigerator in the kitchen especially for Mike's meetings, and it was a ritual that I found amused everyone else in the department, who were usually just waking up with their cups of coffee. Before long, a taxi arrived to take them to Claridges and I was left in the office to take calls and get on with the rest of Mike's work.

The days were varied, busy and long and Mike looked after me by adding extra hours onto my timesheet each week, which made the job financially worthwhile. But as time went by, I was recognising that the position was a responsibility, squeezing my energy, and I was beginning to feel pinned down to office life, pulling me back into the old – which is what I was trying to get away from – and not giving me the freedom I was yearning for.

The first triumph was Crusader House and, being a special occasion, Mike asked me to organise a buffet lunch with plenty of champagne for the whole department in the function rooms at The Ship Tavern, a popular local pub in Holborn. A reward for all the hard work, but whilst everyone was revelling in the celebration of Crusader House, I knew I would have to be back at my desk the next morning, ready to start the whole process all over again by working on the next project - Little Britain.

★

After nine months' absence from Australia, Mike's old secretary finally returned to the UK, needing her old job back, and as I was finding the post heavily demanding in many ways, I was ready to pass the baton over to her.

It had been a worthwhile experience, meeting people involved in the creation of building new parts of London, making history, and I had enjoyed my position there to a certain extent, but my heart was with my dancing. I had gained confidence over the year working at the Chalayan, learning what it was like to entertain, and I was ready to say goodbye to Blythe Dutton as serving in two camps was beginning to limit my objective.

When I got home that evening, satisfied with the thought that I was finally free from the long booking, the phone rang.

"Hello, I want you to come straight away, we have a big party here." It was Ata. I raced to get ready.

When I arrived, the place was packed and I found that the main party who had organised to see me dance was the cast from the Hi-de-Hi! television series, with Ruth Madoc heading the table.

Ata shouted, "Umpa," when I walked through the door and everyone looked round to see who it was. Ruth gave me a lovely smile and having seen her on television, I felt I knew her in a strange way. I kept my lips firmly sealed as I did not want to give my English accent away; I wanted them to think I was Turkish or Arabic, a genuine belly dancer.

"Get ready, get ready," Ata said excitedly. He was in such an exuberant mood that night, which soon became infectious.

"Ladies and gentlemen, we have a young lady all the way from Egypt and her name is Shariffa." Ata put on his favourite piece of Arabic music – Wayak – to start the show.

Both Ata and Pepe were at their best, playing the tambourine and drums as I came out wearing my new costume – bright red and silver, which glistened in the candlelight – and playing my cymbals to a happy crowd, eyes shining, wondering what my next move would be. Tips were coming from everywhere – Ata did not have to show them what to do – and I climbed up onto the chairs and tables, helped up by some of the customers, to everyone's delight.

The atmosphere was wonderful. I felt euphoric as I left the stage.

Ata followed me into the dressing room and shut the door. No words were said. His soft brown eyes looked down at my face. I could hear his breathing, then he swayed slowly towards me and waited, then kissed me on the lips, so gently, so sweetly, only for a second or two. Then he left, closing the door behind him.

★

Ingrid got work for me the next day at a firm of solicitors in London Wall, in the City of London. It was an incredible place. The ground floor was an empty area, made up of shiny white carrara marble, with nothing else around apart from one security guard standing by the escalators that led to the next floor. He did not ask me any questions as I approached the moving staircase and, feeling like a spaceman having passed the OK to carry on towards the spacecraft that was waiting for me at the top of the stairs, I imagined I was about to be taken on a trip to the moon. Every floor contained windows that stretched from top to bottom of the building displaying the stunning views of London. I escalated up and up to the top floor where, along the white shiny corridor, I saw a girl seated behind a white reception desk. She smiled pleasantly whilst booking me in, but my eye was diverted towards the vast views behind her, where the Gherkin was so close that I felt I could almost touch it.

"What are you doing here?" she said with a sweet smile and I apologised for my lack of attention.

"Oh, I was just admiring the view," I replied.

"You are that dancer at the Chalayan," she said eagerly. Then she told me she had seen me dancing a couple of weeks before at the restaurant with friends. But I could not recollect her. I tried to remember the occasion, even though she told me where she had been sitting, who she was with, and what happened during the show - because I never familiarised myself personally with anyone whilst I was dancing, forgetting faces very quickly, mainly acting on impulse as the moment presented itself and never dwelling afterwards on what had happened, relying on the fact that my instincts made the right decision at the time. I could see she was eager for my recollection of the occurrence and, not wanting to disappoint her, I pretended that I suddenly recognised her, adding how much I too enjoyed the evening, putting her mind at rest. She then giggled, realising she had uncovered my secret, that I was also a legal secretary during the daytime, and I became aware of the difficulty of wearing two hats as I was concerned that she might spread the news with her working colleagues about my double life, which sometimes felt too close for comfort.

Perhaps it was because as a secretary I felt an introvert, in my shell and quiet, whereas in my dancing life I was an extrovert, in charge and flamboyant. They were two separate lives and difficult to explain when I was asked questions by those who wanted answers – which I usually tried to avoid.

My fears were unfounded though as the offices were impersonal, and being open-plan, the staff appeared to walk around like zombies with little interaction between each other, and the work was uninspiring enough not to create much discussion between colleagues. I was just another cog in the wheel of motion, unnoticed but necessary for as long as was needed.

But my heart was not sitting in an office that day, it was somewhere else, as I could not stop thinking about what had happened the night before.

Love is like a slow mist that gently descends upon its subjects. It is not recognised at first, until one is surrounded by it, but by then it is too late to do anything about it.

★

The days went by slowly. Ata had not called me or asked me to dance for a party mid-week so I just presumed it had been quiet and could not wait for the weekend. When it arrived, I was so excited about seeing him and got everything ready for the Saturday evening.

As I entered the Chalayan it was full of customers, buoyant and lively, but straight away my heart sank as Pepe told me that Ata would not be coming that night; he had gone to Cyprus for a holiday, not knowing when he was going to return. My first thought was confused as to why he had not said anything about it to me, but Pepe said not to worry as he would still play the drums for me. I continued to be baffled about why Ata had kept me so in the dark about his movements and when I went into the kitchen to see the staff, Hassan the chef added salt to the wound by saying that Ata had gone to Cyprus to look for a wife. Whether it was a joke or not, it cut deep, and what I thought was going to be a joyous evening suddenly felt like an emotional nightmare. Reluctantly I had to pull myself together as I did not want anyone to know my true feelings, and had to quickly understand where I was. With a packed audience waiting to see me dance, Pepe and I knew we could not let them down.

Then to my surprise, little Hussein, who had been hiding, suddenly appeared from nowhere and greeted me with such a warm smile. I wanted to ask him so many questions about his father, but knowing I could not burden such a young boy with my problems, my mind quickly diverted onto other things, even though I could not help feeling that he knew a lot more than he let on.

The show went well even though Ata was not present, and Hussein made a point of shouting 'well done' on my way back to the dressing room. He sounded so grown-up and his comment was so uplifting from one so young. Soon after there was a knock on the door, and I allowed Hussein in.

"Why do you do this dance?" he asked, looking up at me and waiting for an answer. He knew there was something I was not sharing with him. He wanted an answer and I tried to ignore his question by pretending to be busy. "Why do you do this dance?" he asked again. There was silence whilst he waited for a reply.

I tried to evade the subject, thinking he would ask me another question in a moment or two, but he persisted by asking me again, showing he had no intention of giving up. I thought that if I gave him an answer, he would tell his father and that I could be made fun of amongst the staff besides the customers, and I was in a dilemma as to how to respond to him.

He was looking at me with big wondrous eyes, still waiting for an answer. He was not going to let go. I knew I could not get out if it and decided there was nothing I could do but to be open with him.

"OK, I will tell you," I said, "but only if you promise never to tell your father."

He sensed the severity of my concern and promised me that he would never tell his father. I asked him to promise me again to make sure he really understood my anxiety. He demonstrated emphatically that he would never tell his father if I told him the truth and as I decided to rely on my intuition that I could trust him, I began to explain my philosophy to him.

I told him that I believed in life after death. That we all have a spiritual journey with a purpose and a destiny to fulfil. Our Fate is planned beforehand and we are given Free Will to choose whether to accept that Fate or not. If we stray or wander from the Fate that was intended, then life will repeat the same old lessons over and over, like the lapping of the sea, until we are ready to reach that higher self. We are not here purely for our own egos and our own material wealth; there is another purpose and we can either listen to that purpose or push it aside for another day. It is up to us when we are ready to listen to our inner selves and it does not matter how long it takes; there is no time limit. Our conscience is our guide as to how we rule our lives, with an inner sense of what is right and what is wrong. Once we reach that higher self, we cannot retract into our old selves and enjoy the ignorance we once knew - as our conscience would have risen to a different level where there is no going back.

It was a lot for a little boy to take in and Hussein listened intently as though he understood every word but he was still waiting for an answer. I could not delay it any longer.

"OK," I said. "I am doing the dance because I feel it is part of my karma and that Fate has guided me to this point."

I looked at him, expecting him to giggle and dash out of the door to tell everyone, but he did not.

"Don't you dare tell your father," I begged him.

He gave me a knowing smile, twisting his lip as he does, understanding I had shared something special with him. "I promise I will never tell my father," he said solemnly.

★

Ata still had not returned from Cyprus over the next weeks and not only were the staff unaware of when he would be back in the

UK, but also the customers were wondering what had happened to him. It was an enigma and I felt at a loss that he had not been in touch.

After one of my shows, a customer at the Chalayan told me I danced well and informed me about The Divan, a Turkish club in Lewisham, where there could be the possibility of getting a job as a dancer and gave me their number. I had a strong desire to experience other places and work further afield so I took the opportunity to phone them and the owner asked me to pop round to meet him.

At 11pm it was not too difficult to find in Lewisham, as the bright lights of the club were advertised outside the premises against the darkness of the closed shops next door, but for all the razzmatazz surrounding its identification, I sensed an eeriness about the place; there was a noticeable lack of street lighting and apart from a few cars parked outside, there was nobody about.

I entered the club, adjusting my eyes to the dim candlelight that reflected the layout of the interior, and was immediately struck by the dense smell of cigarette smoke stifling the air. Groups of single men filled the tables enjoying each other's company, whilst others were engaged with pretty ladies, clinging onto them for support. A small band occupied a corner of the stage playing Turkish music to a nostalgic audience, some dreamily twirling their worry beads to the melodies well known to them, satisfying a longing for those who had strong memories of the past.

I asked a Turkish waiter if I could see the owner whereupon he gave me a strange look, but led me to a table where four men were seated, playing backgammon, drinking and smoking.

I introduced myself, telling them that I was a belly dancer and was interested in working at their club. The owner, Mahmut, asked me to sit down and join them. "How much you charge?" he asked. I gave him a reasonable price as I was honest about my experience, explaining I had been working in a Turkish Cypriot restaurant for nearly two years but had not danced with a live band before, having only worked with tapes that I had edited myself for small audiences. He told me he already had a dancer, Turkish and experienced, but that she was leaving at the end of the week and he would be needing a replacement. He then asked if I would watch the dancer's show that night to see if I could take her place, which I happily agreed to do.

Being unfamiliar with Turkish music and the various melodies, I learnt that the oud was an instrument made up of eleven to fifteen strings, which had a similarity to the lute and was often accompanied by the saz – or bağlama – with its long neck and similiar sound to the violin, and the clarinet and drums had prominent parts to play attended by a small piano.

The history of Turkish music, both classical and folk, goes back to the Ottoman Empire, with contributions from Greek, Armenian, Kurdish, Albanian and Jewish influences. Stories reflect on religion, love and war and are handed down from generation to generation over the years. Most of the customers had grown to love the tunes from childhood, knowing them off by heart and mouthing some of the words whilst washing down their heartfelt emotions with a glass of raki. I knew the power that music can have but I felt at a disadvantage not having heard the melodies before and began to feel a bit out of my depth.

The general rota for the programme was that an unfamiliar Turkish singer would start the show, followed by the belly dancer before the celebrity singer, who was specially brought over from Turkey, to finish the show.

In the early hours of the morning, Zehra, the Turkish dancer, finally emerged. I was waiting for her appearance as I had not seen a dancer from Turkey before. She was tall with beautiful black hair flowing around her slim body, but it was noticeable that she had undergone a cosmetic breast enlargement, which she must have felt was necessary for her profession. She was wearing the skimpiest of sequinned costumes as she floated around the stage.

I watched as she eventually parted from the band, playing her cymbals, to slowly edge towards the tables, manoeuvring herself from one customer to the next. She gently flirted in a salacious and intimate way around her victims, who inevitably became entrapped in her spell, showing their appreciation by showering her with notes and slipping them all around her costume. Some of her gestures appeared slinky with a sense of eroticism about them, which I found difficult to place within the dance as I knew it to be, and I became aware that there were certain differences of style between the Arabic and Turkish ways of portraying the belly dance which made me wonder whether I was suitable for the position.

Ata had shown me how to deal with his customers, who were more family-orientated – the dancer could acquire a touch of comedy to boost the show, make a fuss of someone on their birthday, or tease a wife's husband or girlfriend's partner for simple light fun – but this was different.

I heard her play the finger cymbals throughout the show, which I felt comfortable with, having played them myself at the Chalayan for certain lengths of time, although I recognised it was more of a Turkish tradition than an Arabic one. Arabic dancers remained on the stage to play the cymbals to a special piece of music composed for that purpose and would eventually lay them down by the band after use. But Turkish dancers play the cymbals whilst dancing during the whole show.

In this case, Zehra had cleverly mastered how to play her cymbals around the customers, by enticing them to give her tips. They were like second nature to her as the customers were drawn in to listen to her story. The band would follow and keep the rhythm of the melody for as long as it took until the dancer acknowledged that she had finished her mission by returning to the stage to finalise the show. Tips were her bread and butter, not only for herself but for the band who were reliant on their half share. I had a hard act to follow as the Turkish dancer was good at it.

After Zehra had left the stage, the owner approached me and asked if I could come in the following night to show them what I could do. I told Mahmut how I saw a difference in our styles, that I was more of an Arabic dancer than a Turkish one, but he did not seem to mind so I agreed to his offer as I thought I had nothing to lose.

When I returned the next night, I heard that Zehra had already left and was on her way back to Turkey. The tables were busy with customers waiting to be entertained and whilst the first singer of the evening, Gemil, was performing, the owner came over to me and asked me to get ready.

I went upstairs, where there was a small room that I could change in. It felt unpleasant and somewhat unsavoury. There was an old worn carpet on the floor that looked like it had been there for years, curtains at the windows too torn to close for privacy and an unused shabby wardrobe tucked away in the corner of the room. Dirty blankets lingered on an old bed which reeked of human odour, and I felt the room had been used for illicit purposes. I was beginning to acquaint myself with the hidden dangers behind the scenes and began to consider my safety there for the first time, realising that I should take charge of my own naivety.

I decided to wear my bright gold costume that I had made myself with long gold strands hanging symmetrically from the hips. I carefully fitted my finger cymbals on my fingers and lightly attached the veil to the inside of my belt to flimsily cover me, as I waited for my cue.

I could hear my name being announced, with the beginning

section of my music – 'Azziza' – already in play, but as the piece has a long stretch at the beginning, I had plenty of time to descend the stairs and wait until it was time for me to approach the stage.

At first, the music sounded unfamiliar to me and difficult to recognise as the tiny band played my chosen piece, and I had to thoroughly concentrate whilst playing my finger cymbals to match the beat as I tried to follow the melody.

I arrived on the stage twirling my veil, which was eventually allowed to drop to the ground. I was hoping to lull the audience into my story until it was time for me to venture towards the customers, playing my cymbals as I approached the tables. I had to rely on my instinct to choose the right customer from each table to act as my patriarch, who was proud enough to flaunt his affluence, power and masculinity by showing his colleagues he could treat me well by placing a handsome tip in my costume. My first choice was paramount for success as the other customers would hopefully follow suit. For a split second, I wished Ata was there to guide me towards those he knew would be men of means and able to look after me, but alas, this time I was on my own.

Suddenly, I caught eye contact with one of the customers who persuaded me to get up on his chair and then helped me up onto the table, where he neatly tucked notes of all denominations around my costume. I had chosen wisely as his colleagues followed his procedure so as not to look disrespectful, smiling, flirting, sharing a childlike sense of fun between them. Tips were placed in the hipster belt and bra until it was time to move onto the next table and again, I was helped on and off chairs and tables as the band played to suit the timing of my movements. Waiters collected fallen notes, placing them back into my costume, while the music lingered to give plenty of time for me to move from one table to the next.

When I finished with all the tables and felt everyone had

had their fun, I made my way back to the stage to prepare for the final stages of the dance. The drummer had never practised with me before, and it was not easy to follow his drum solo, but I made a reasonable effort at the unrehearsed attempt, which was followed by a shimmer and a short spin. To finish, I gave a tiny bow with my right hand lightly touching my forehead before leaving to a good applause, and I ran up the stairs triumphant, knowing they had accepted me.

I sat down and carefully counted the notes that were stuffed in my costume, knowing the band had an idea of how much I had made that night and were expecting their cut on my return. I had heard whispers that if the band did not receive their half, or felt the dancer was not looking after them, the dancer would not only lose her job but be labelled with a bad name for future work. I always gave a bit more than half so that there could be no repercussions as the actual experience of working in the club was far more valuable to me than the receiving of tips, as I was fortunate enough to have the backup of a second income from my secretarial work.

Fully aware of my duty on my return, I handed over a half share of the tips to the leader of the band who, without a smile, wearing dark glasses, managed to give a slight nod as though their half was expected and not given as a gift. I then made my way to sit down at one of the staff tables when Mahmut came over to talk to me.

He offered me the job. The hours were from midnight to 5.00am, six nights a week. The first drink was on the house but thereafter drinks were to be paid for. He preferred that I did not mix with the customers and I was not to leave the club before the final singer had finished. I was absolutely delighted they had accepted me to dance there and stayed the rest of the evening to listen to the celebrity singer take to the stage.

The audience had been waiting all night to hear her sing,

acknowledging their appreciation by lavishly tipping her. They needed to share their memories with her and she did not let them down, singing their favourites, reeling off one after another to a dedicated, captive audience. She was a prima donna and it was apparent she was adored by everybody.

I left around 4.30am into the night air, with not a soul about, in the hope that I could get home in time to grab an hour or two of sleep before the agency's phone call later that morning to send me out to work that day.

★

Ata finally returned from his holidays. I had been at the club for over a month whilst he had been away. It felt such a long time since I last saw him, and as he looked so well after his break in Cyprus I wondered if he had missed me. He greeted me, shouting out loud that he had so everyone could hear, but I was beginning to question whether he really meant it – although I was relieved to see he had not brought back a new wife.

He, too, wondered if I had missed him, because when I told him I was working in a Turkish club, he did not seem too pleased at first, giving me the impression that he did not want to share me. I explained to Ata that as they had already offered me the job whilst he was away, I could not leave them in limbo until he returned, and that I had already informed the owner of my loyalty towards him whereupon Mahmut had shown his respect by offering me flexible hours to fit in with him. Ata was placated by my words, hearing where my priorities lay, and then wondered if he knew the owner. There was obviously a hidden respect between the two men, both being in the same business, but when I further reassured him where my heart lay, that I never wanted to leave the Chalayan and that I was happy there, he finally relented, knowing I was not going to stray.

★

Whilst I was working late nights at the club, Ingrid made sure that I did not get more than one or two days' secretarial work at the most a week, keeping it to a minimum as I was also on call for dancing at early evening parties at the Chalayan, which meant that I did not always arrive on time at the Turkish club. Even though Mahmut had accepted my hours, I often wondered if the rest of the staff and the band resented my time-keeping as they had a certain routine to follow, which meant Gemil, the young Turkish singer, would have to wait for my arrival before starting the show.

As the weeks and months at the club passed by, I began to get to know Gemil quite well. He would join me at one of the staff tables to share aimless banter until the early hours of the morning whilst the celebrity singer from Turkey completed her show.

He lived in a flat nearby that he shared with his girlfriend and seemed happy to be over here in the UK, although he was looking forward to returning to Turkey to see his family for a holiday. He was good enough to translate some of the Turkish songs into English for me, describing the origin of the story connected to the tune, which helped me familiarise myself with some of the music. I found most of the storylines unique but sometimes overpowering in their content, quite different from the essence of the pop songs I had grown to know in the UK. Generally, though, the themes in their music were usually about religion, love and war, with the complicated scenarios surrounding them!

When he began to trust me a little more, knowing I did not share our chatter with others, he told me that the owner had been visited a few times by the police who had been investigating any wrongdoing on the premises, which caused Mahmut to clean up his act as he had been under pressure for some time to stop the associations the previous dancer had been having with some of the customers there, making it a difficult problem for him. Gemil told me it was the main reason he had to get rid of her, and why he did not want me to sit and mix with the customers or get to know any of them personally. I did not persist with further questions on the topic as Gemil had already verified what I assumed had been going on in the changing room upstairs, but thought how lucky I was, having the job after Zehra, as I would not have accepted the position otherwise.

After I was put in the picture about what was going on there, I still could not tell Gemil about the problems I was experiencing with the head waiter, who kept giving me strange looks every now and again, making it apparent he was not happy with my being there. From the first day I had arrived at the club I sensed he disliked my presence, but as time moved on, I was finding his attitude quite disconcerting. I tried to shrug it off, but even though I tucked myself away on a staff table, keeping myself to myself, it did not stop his gaze from heading in my direction – a cold, blank stare with the definite intention of trying to unnerve me. There I was, surrounded by people yet isolated by the intense strange looks from that one man. He knew, as I knew, that I would be in a more vulnerable position if I told anyone about it. He had me cornered. What it was about, I had no idea, but I felt threatened by him nonetheless.

In time, I found myself becoming separated and detached from everyone else in the club apart from Gemil. The band, never joined me at the staff tables during their breaks to communicate or talk to me, which I knew was not the case with the previous dancer, having noticed there had been a very close bond between them.

As Gemil and I talked through the early hours of the morning, he gradually enlightened me about some of the misdemeanours the head waiter had caused in the past towards various staff members working in the club. He explained that one evening, after I had left, the head waiter was caught up in a brawl in the street outside with a member of the band over tips. Apparently, the band member was lucky enough to escape with just cuts and bruises, but that it could have been far worse. Gemil had heard of one band member having his knuckles broken in a fight a few months back – a tragic injury for a professional musician.

Hearing about that incident obviously concerned me, but when Gemil told me that the head waiter had been involved in an association with Zehra, everything suddenly fell into place.

I began to realise the danger I was in.

As I was showing no intention of going down the same road as the previous dancer, having personal connections with some of the customers, I realised that my non-contribution of earnings from those associations was causing resentment between the head waiter and members of the band who were missing out on backhand tips from the process. Whatever it was, I sensed tension growing in the club and felt the head waiter disapproved of my late arrival sometimes, believing I was getting preferential treatment, when he himself, had to work long drawn-out hours on perhaps low wages, and begrudged the fact that as a single woman, I could look after myself without having to succumb to other pursuits, which would have been useful as another form of revenue for him.

The owner had to try and show the authorities he was exempt from any illegal practices at the club, and I could not tell whether he was aware of the silent pressure being put upon me by his staff, but I was determined not to get involved with any illicit practices at the club in order to keep a job.

After a short while, thinking heavily about my position there and not feeling thoroughly secure, I decided to call it a day, and the next night approached Mehmet to tell him that even though I had enjoyed working with him over the last four months, I felt it was the right time for me to leave. He did not show much expression as I gave him the news, accepting my notice in good grace, and we parted in reasonable harmony with his understanding that he would be needing to find another dancer to fill my place.

★

I was free from the shackles of the all-night job at the club, realising how physically demanding it had been working nights, with the disorientation of fitting in with a different routine. It took time to return to the familiar circuit of office hours, having to change sleeping patterns and other habits, which was never easy to adapt to at first.

I was offered an opportunity to travel by car from London once a fortnight with a small band of three Turkish musicians to dance at the Istanbul Delight, a Turkish Restaurant in the centre of Colchester. The owner, Mehmet, looked after us when we arrived by treating us to good food and wine before the show and paid us well for making the journey. I danced more than once as it was always fully booked for our arrival, making good tips that I happily shared with the band. After the show we travelled back to London in the early hours of the morning and on those occasions, I was lucky to get back home in time to grab a few hours' sleep before arriving at work the next morning.

Those same musicians had a three-night booking at a Turkish restaurant in Huddersfield in Yorkshire and I was asked to share the venue with them as the owner thought it would be a unique experience for his customers, who had never seen a live performance from a belly dancer before.

We travelled by car on the long journey to Huddersfield,

arriving late to stay with friends of the musicians, where I had my own little room, which I was grateful for as everyone else had to share space on put-you-ups. It was all a bit cramped, but everyone got on with one another and was looking forward to the evenings ahead, when they would listen to old Turkish melodies and watch the show.

The restaurant, Ata Turk, was in the heart of Huddersfield, and the owner, Erdinch, squeezed a place for us in the corner of the main dining area as a small stage. There were a few Turkish customers but the clientele was mainly a mixture of hardened northerners and Europeans who were unfamiliar with Turkish traditions but keen to enjoy the cuisine, hear the live music and watch the show. When it came to my time to dance and leave the stage after I had dropped my veil, the waiters flurried around to escort me onto the tables they knew I would be valued the most, where Turkish families tipped me well, and the drummer isolated himself from the band to follow me around and personally ad lib for me as I danced around the tables. For those customers who had never seen a belly dancer before, I brought in a touch of comedy, enticing them to join in, with an odd kiss on the cheek for the oldest amongst the group. They clapped their hands, trying to sing in harmony with the musicians, and occasionally even dared to place a tip in my costume which caused a loud cheer from the other Turkish families. The band had not seen me work in that mode before, mixing comedy with the more traditional side of the dance, but it worked, and everyone joined in and enjoyed themselves.

On our last night, after the show the owner Erdinch joined us as we visited Johnny's, the main nightclub in the centre of town, where we were fortunate to meet the actors from the *Last of the Summer Wine* series on television – Peter Sallis, Bill Owen and Peter Fyffe who were enjoying a drink and sharing chatter with the general public after a day's filming in the area – which was a lovely way to end our enjoyable visit to the unique town of Huddersfield.

★

I was dancing once a fortnight at the Istanbul Delight in Colchester, the Chalayan at the weekends, and performing for the odd assignments outside London when Ingrid asked me to go to Lee Bolton Lee, later to become Lee Bolton Monier-Williams – a very old, established firm of solicitors at No.1 The Sanctuary, Westminster, SW1, a prestigious part of London. It was a beautiful old building with a grand staircase monopolising the centre of the structure, winding round and round, climbing to the top into the attic areas, which was in constant use as there were no lifts to facilitate the staff.

I was introduced to Mr Field on the second floor, a pleasant, elderly gentleman, head of his department in Trust and Probate. He occupied an impressive office surrounded with oak bookcases filled with lever arch files displaying the identity of aristocratic families and other household names that had been elegantly handwritten in thick black ink on the outside of the binders that were in process for probate. His office overlooked College Garden, the private grounds of Westminster Abbey, once owned by the Benedictine monks nine hundred years ago, with a quaint fountain sitting as a centre-piece in the middle of a charming plot of land – where medicinal herbs and foods were once grown for the monks of the Abbey.

The somewhat crumbling stone precinct wall surrounding the gardens is one of the oldest structures in London, dating back to the late 1300s, and Westminster School, within the grounds, was built in 1560 by Elizabeth I. Here a further two individual gardens, Little Cloisters and Garth, were also erected by the monks. Each of the four saint statues placed in the centre of the gardens was carved in 1686 by sculptor Arnold Quellin.

Such an oasis of peace amidst the flurry of heavy traffic that relentlessly passed the other side of the building en route from the Houses of Parliament, travelling alongside the Abbey into Victoria Street.

I was shown where I would be sitting for the next couple of weeks in a room across the corridor that Mr Field's permanent secretary had occupied over the years. A woolly cardigan of hers was heavily wrapped around the typist's chair, demonstrating to the newcomer that she still inhabited her position there and emphasising that she would be back at a moment's notice to retrieve her place if anyone thought otherwise.

The woolly cardigan suddenly made me recoil. I could not touch it and asked someone in the office to take it away for me as I had a phobia of woolly cardigans with buttons. I was grateful when one of the secretaries kindly removed it for me in such a pleasant way, particularly as she showed a certain bemusement about my request in her expression at first - as I hoped not to cause any animosity whilst working there.

I was placed by the window, overlooking Westminster Abbey – built by Edward the Confessor in 1065 – and the view immediately took my breath away. I could watch everything that went on. My eyes were constantly diverted from my work to observe the scene outside. Coachloads of tourists arriving in their hundreds from different lands introduced themselves to the marshalls at the gate, who greeted everyone with welcoming smiles as they entered the Abbey. Remembrance Day Sunday was looming at the weekend and poppies had been placed in the grounds to commemorate those lost soldiers who had bravely fought for our country over two World Wars.

During the week the Duke of Edinburgh arrived. The doors of his Daimler were opened for him by the heavily cloaked marshalls, and the Archbishops bowed and scraped around him as he entered the Abbey gates to walk about the grounds. There he sauntered along with his entourage following, observing the little crosses that had been placed symmetrically and neatly on the lawn outside the Abbey, with officials and members of the public silently watching close by. There was plenty of activity with journalists running around, jostling for space to get the best pictures for their newspapers the next day. The Duke was nodding his head frequently, returning odd words back to the dignitaries who were advising him of some of the names written on the crosses as they slowly moved one by one along the grass verges. The Church bells pealed but were muffled with a leather pad strapped to one side of the clapper ball to create a solemnity of sound. There was a sense of togetherness and acceptance that man was not alone in his fear of death. This was the hour and time to share in gratitude and thanks to those who sacrificed their lives for King or Queen and country, never to be forgotten.

Later, around 4.30pm, the signed post had to be taken downstairs, but to save time and effort for the staff, a strong wicker basket had been installed at the centre of the staircase with pulleys and ropes that elevated from one floor to the next, allowing secretaries to place their signed letters and documents into the container saving them from having to run up and down the stairs to deliver the post. Once the basket landed on the ground floor, the staff below hurriedly removed the correspondence, taking it to the post room to be weighed, stamped, sealed and despatched, before elevating the basket to the top of the building again, repeating the process for the latecomers to add their post until it was all collected for the day. It was unique in its style, perhaps eccentric, but it worked so well.

★

Ata called. He said the restaurant was quiet and wondered if I would like to pop in and say hello.

I had finished work. I was at home relaxing but thought it would be a great opportunity to see everyone there whilst not under stress for a change, having to catch conversation when the place was heaving with customers, and not being kept in the dressing room until I was called to dance.

I told him I was on my way.

It felt strange entering the restaurant without being needed to dance and noticing the empty tables with no-one there to contribute to the atmosphere I was generally accustomed to. Soft music was playing in the background to keep the staff company whilst busy in the kitchen and I saw Ata was seated at one of the tables.

"Hello," he barked in a responsive way. "Sit down. Would you like coffee?" I sat down to join him. Then he told me he had just taken Hussein to the airport to join other pupils who were going on a school trip to Paris for a couple of days. "I'm going to see a friend in Edgware. Would you like to come with me, and I can take you home afterwards?"

Ata closed the restaurant for the night, with the staff leaving early, and he drove me to a small Turkish café in Edgware. On our arrival outside the café, I heard Turkish music playing loudly from the pavement while Ata carefully parked the car, and as we entered through a doorway of beads, we saw a few customers seated around the tables with their eyes glistening from having knocked back a few glasses of raki. The staff appeared delighted that Ata had taken the trouble to call round to see them and they all hugged one another as though they knew each other well, like long-lost friends.

Ata spoke in his Mother tongue for a change, which I found fascinating, and he introduced me to each member of staff individually. They pulled up chairs for us to sit around a large table and the youngest in the group brought a varied collection of mezes and wine to the table, making every effort to make us feel welcome. Ata was enjoying the camaraderie between them, laughing out loud in places and taking the stage by keeping them amused, and even though I could not fully understand what they were saying and was not able to join in the chatter, they wanted me to know that I was accepted as one of the group, especially as I was Ata's guest.

The evening wore on and as it was getting late, Ata decided it was time for us to leave, and with everyone saying their heartfelt goodbyes to one another, we got into the car to get home.

On our way, we passed the restaurant and he explained how he got up early in the mornings to get what he needed from the markets to make sure that everything was fresh for the kitchen the next day, and being one of the reasons for having such good clientele. He started to tell me that he learnt his trade from his parents in Cyprus who owned a large taverna in Nicosia, where they catered for plenty of parties and big weddings, and it became relevant he had been brought up in a life of entertainment, learning the business from an early age.

Life as a restaurateur sounded invigorating, even though extremely hard work with long hours and Ata emphasised the enjoyment he got from the satisfaction of seeing his customers having a good time. It was a life I was unfamiliar with, creating more of a challenge than I had envisaged and bearing a lot more responsibility than I had imagined, but it sounded much more rewarding than finishing a day as a secretary in a legal office.

Eventually he stopped the car. Everything went quiet. We had arrived outside my home. He leant across to help me open the door. It would not open. His face was so close. We kissed. Passionately.

★

Christmas started early in restaurants and I hoped I could get some bookings as there were many parties at that time of the year. A popular Greek restaurant called Kantara in the heart of Covent Garden gave me a six-week booking to dance for their busy lunchtime customers from Monday to Saturday. There were two floors with the basement area pre-booked for office parties, and because the atmosphere had a slight similarity to the Chalayan, I felt quite capable of managing both events.

At the same time, Ingrid at the agency, having heard about my heavy schedule but not wanting to lose my services, was able to find me a unique position in entertainment law, working for a friendly firm of solicitors nearby, where the senior partner agreed to accept my precarious hours, allowing me to have a two-hour lunch break with a day off a week. It meant that I could carry on with my exploits as a dancer not only during the day but also at night, which was an offer I could not refuse even though it meant having to carry my costume with my other belongings to the office each day ready for the lunchtime shows.

Whilst answering the phone at the solicitors, calls came through from well-known sports commentators Harry Carpenter and Brian Moore, and other presenters from the BBC including famous actors and actresses, needing legal advice when to my utter surprise a well-spoken gentleman told me his name was Peter O'Toole. I could not keep the excitement to myself, telling him he was my heartthrob, especially after seeing him in *Lawrence of Arabia*, and after hearing my enthusiasm, he softened his tone at the other end of the line, clearly flattered, until I was able to put him through to the solicitor who was waiting for the call.

When I arrived at the Kantara around 12.15pm, they asked me to change in a tiny room near the kitchen, which was icy cold as it was surrounded by fridges and freezers containing all their meat produce and other edibles. Bottles of wine lined the walls on the shelves above, but they were no solace to the biting cold that emerged from the refrigerators and after I had changed into my costume, I clung onto my thick winter coat until the last minute. Fortunately they did not leave me too long, and when I heard my music I had forgotten about the cold as it was time to dance, firstly on the ground floor, around the customers – office folk, tourists and the general public dining, some confused as to why I was there, others loving the notoriety. Waiters planted notes in my costume to show the customers what was expected of them and in between the meze, plates of moussaka and tight table arrangements, I managed to entertain the public in any way I could.

When I finished, I ran back into the tiny changing room for a quick breather before my next show in the basement area, where there were business parties and office groups celebrating that time of year, with plenty of wine and beer flowing. Although well organised by the waiters, the tradition of the dance got lost in all the enthusiasm, fun and laughter as I stepped from one table onto the next.

By the time I had completed the second show after a quick change, I dashed back to the office, arriving at approximately 2.15pm, to sit at my desk as though nothing had happened. I found it strange that no one questioned where I had been or queried why I had taken such a long break, as I knew the senior partner would not have told them, but they just carried on with their daily routine, expecting me to do the same. At first I had difficulties fitting into such a strict disciplined regime straight after my lunchtime antics, but once I put the earplugs in my ears, placed my fingers on the keys and started the foot pedal, I somehow automatically went into autopilot until the end of the day.

★

During Christmas week, the Kantara asked me to take an afternoon off from my day job as they had a special function to cater for and I arrived at the restaurant around 3.30pm. To my surprise, I was confronted by a burley policeman at the door stopping me from entering the premises. "Your name, please," he asked sternly. I told him and he said, "Yes, they described you quite well, you can go in." I wondered what it was all about as I went downstairs and edged my way to the tiny changing room by the kitchen, only to find another dancer in there. Apparently she had already danced, and she was changing back into her everyday clothes, telling me that I was to be the last of the four dancers that afternoon for a group of people who had booked the whole restaurant for the rest of the day for their private function. Then she told me they were all from the Ministry of Defence, thus the need for a policeman at the entrance door to bar the general public from attending, and it all began to make sense.

I enjoyed a glass of house white Soave whilst changing and when I heard my music, I entered the public arena, playing my cymbals to a room filled with men dressed in City suits, one or two still clutching their red boxes containing confidential papers whilst showing their versatility by balancing their desired drink in the other hand.

They were standing in groups, no one was sitting down; it seemed more like a buffet affair and strange to dance around people who were not seated. But the atmosphere was exhilarating. Laughter was prevalent. They appeared entrepreneurial, with a well-travelled air about them, a worldly crowd who knew how to be and what to do, and I felt safe and protected in their company. They were obviously public school, a well-behaved crowd who treated me with respect, with manners beyond reproach, some daring to place large tips in my costume whilst others smiled charmingly as I passed by. One or two sported rosy cheeks from over-drinking, whilst others looked on in a soberly way, witnessing the reactions of their colleagues as I gracefully edged for tips.

I finished with a shimmer, a short spin and a simple bow before returning to change, when the owner of the Kantara came to see me in the changing room to say that they had invited me to join them for a drink afterwards if I was interested.

I was delighted to accept their offer as I was fascinated to meet them in more normal circumstances than dancing around them, and was escorted to meet a group of men in the middle of the room who openly introduced themselves, giving me their personal names and offering me a glass of champagne, which I happily accepted. They originally thought that I was a genuine belly dancer, which pleased me, but when they realised I was English, they wondered why I was involved in the dance as a profession. That was a difficult question to answer other than my emphasis on the fascination for the dance itself. Then when they heard I was also a legal secretary, a profession I managed to fit in during the day, the door was open to a string of jokes and leg-pulling that carried on for most of the afternoon. One of the phrases they kept repeating was that they had signed the Official Secrets Act, which always created uncontrollable bursts of laughter every time they said it, knowing they were not allowed to say more than they should. Whether that was because I was asking tricky questions or because they were avoiding telling me much about themselves, I could not tell, but I kept them amused pretending that I too had signed the Official Secrets Act on many occasions whilst temping in Her Majesty's Government Offices in Whitehall, and was therefore unable to verify my having two occupations or answer all their questions. This caused further laughter that carried on all through the afternoon. It was one of those magical occasions that I will always treasure.

Before we parted, some of them offered me their personal cards with the intention of my visiting the Ministry of Defence, where I would have been shown around and taken out for lunch, but sadly I never took them up on the offer, not because I did not want to, but because my life seemed so busy at the time that I did not have the opportunity to organise it.

★

I was happy. Everything was wonderful with my shows at the Chalayan, dancing at the Kantara at lunchtime and bookings every night for six weeks over the Christmas period for three big Italian restaurants along Exhibition Road in London, owned by an Italian proprietor, Lorenzo.

La Pergola was the first venue. It was a massive place where I was expected to dance on the ground floor around the tables, playfully begging for tips, but as belly dancing was not their culture being an Italian restaurant, they were completely unaware of what I was begging for! As the waiters were not able to help, I used a touch of comedy in my shows for the Christmas fun as I went around the tables, where customers enjoyed seeing their spouse, boyfriend or family friends participate in the atmosphere.

Downstairs there was a large dance area, where I performed on the stage with an announcement from the DJ and the audience encircled around me to watch the show.

To save changing my costume from one venue to the next, I wore a long coat to cover me as I walked along Exhibition Road to the next restaurant, Vecchiomondo, which was only a few hundred yards away. My show there was based on the same principle as the previous restaurant – dancing upstairs around the tables and then on the stage downstairs.

Further along the road was the baby of the group, La Belvista, a smaller restaurant where a lone guitarist played for most of the evening until I arrived, when one of my tapes playing Arabic music would be used to dance around the customers, lasting around fifteen minutes. Whilst there, I was often told by a member of staff that someone called Ada or Ata had called to check whether I had left to arrive at the Chalayan and after the show I returned the call to say that I had completed the circuit and was on my way.

I kept that tight schedule for over six years during the six-week Christmas period, where everything had to be timed perfectly. Being a sole entertainer automatically created its own difficulties, especially when the waiters and DJs at the Italian restaurants changed regularly, not knowing the procedure. It was important for me to acquaint myself with various members of staff before each show to make them aware of what I was about to do and explain that I would need their attention when waiting in the wings so the DJ could put my music on before I entered the stage. There was always so much going on and it was not always easy to catch a waiter's eye to let them know I was changed and ready to be on the stage. With the timing of each show being so essential to appearing at the next engagement on time, needing the full co-operation of everyone around me for that purpose could be quite stressful although the exhilaration I felt from seeing the customers enjoying themselves, looking as though they were having a good time, made up for any difficulties I might have had.

★

During that time of year, I would often be asked to dance at one-off events, which I tried to fit in besides my scheduled venues when I was surprised by a call from a senior partner in a firm of solicitors down Chancery Lane where I once worked, who said he had kept his promise in keeping my secret about my evening activities from other members of the staff but as it was Christmas, would I do a special show at a restaurant he had chosen as a surprise for his firm? He believed my appearance could be a 'Christmas cracker'!

I was impressed that the dour man I had worked for, who had never shown much expression or enthusiasm for anything other than legal matters, was keen to see me dance and told him I was delighted with the idea but that I would have to seek the restaurant's permission before I could perform. He gave me the details and name of the restaurant in Oxford Circus so that I could visit them and arrange for the show to take place. It was a small Greek family concern who said they were happy to let me dance for the party and promised me they would not let on to anyone who I was when I arrived so that it could remain a surprise.

It was suggested that I be invited as a guest to join the firm in the way of a reunion of staff for a Christmas party and when I arrived, everyone appeared pleased to see me, asking me how I was and chatting about old times. Then they told me they were looking forward to the belly dancer that night, who had been laid on specially for the occasion. I believed they had no idea who the dancer was going to be that evening and, keeping my part of the bargain, I professed that I too was looking forward to the show.

After dinner, one of the waiters came to tell me that I had a telephone call, and could I take it at the back of the restaurant? It was my cue to change and I hoped the party would not guess what I was doing whilst I was absent from the table. I pretended it was going to be a lengthy telephone call and that I might even have to miss the show.

It was a tiny room to change in with insufficient space, but I managed and heard my name being announced – 'Shariffa'.

My music began and as I danced out into the dining area, I do not think I had ever seen such a bevy of strange expressions on people's faces as I had on that occasion. Their mouths were wide open and their eyes screwed in disbelief as the penny slowly dropped as they recognised who I was. Eventually I floated towards the senior partner who I had worked for as a temp and he allowed me to sit on his lap for a short while, which caused hoots of laughter and giggles all around us, before I got him up from the table to copy some of my movements in front of the office crowd.

There was not a dry eye in the house. It was one of those special occasions that could not easily be repeated. It also showed how trusted the senior partner had been in keeping my secret in confidence from the staff for all those months, which of course added to the suprise.

*

After Christmas, it was a good time to catch up with old friends. Colin wanted to hear about my experiences at the Turkish club, which I told him about in as much detail as I could although I kept quiet about some of the difficulties I had experienced there as I did not want him to be concerned about my welfare. We were still good friends, although not seeing one another as much as we had in the past, but I noticed he deliberately avoided asking me questions about Ata or the Chalayan, which I was grateful for as I knew I would have felt most uncomfortable if he had.

Also, as I had not attended Selwa's classes for a while, the short break gave me a chance to meet up with my two dancing friends, Helen and Joannie, who also wanted to catch up on the news. Joannie, though, was continuing to have difficulty mastering the camel walk and, as I had promised to help her personally, she invited me round to her house to show her where she was going wrong.

The camel walk is like a slow wave from the knees up to the torso. If one sat on a camel, one would automatically display the movement, but without the camel it is not as easy!

Joannie was very light in stature with blonde hair swept back like a bob behind her ears, with serene features and a gentle nature. She lived in a large house at the back of Barkers, off Kensington High Street, with a live-in maid occupying the basement of the house – not forgetting a white Mercedez, which was one of her cars parked outside.

When I arrived at her door, Joannie answered to let me in and showed me around the house. It was exquisitely furnished with soft fabrics and a display of antiques, but what caught my eye most of all was a little room at the back of the house that she had created herself depicting a kasbah influence, with tapestries covering the walls, tiny mirrors reflected on plush cushions strewn on ankle-high sofa beds, and glittering stones that sparkled like jewels hanging from the chandeliers and surrounding fabrics. There was also the heavy aroma of jasmine burning from the incense sticks placed in novelty holders at each corner of the room. It was like Aladdin's cave, a special closet of dreams, fantasies and magical whispers, a place where one could be alone, yet not alone. Slightly hidden away in a specially made shrine was an ordinary television screen, where she played videos of belly dancers from all over the world.

She took me downstairs to the kitchen area, where I was treated to a light salmon lunch, washed down with a chilled glass of Savignon Blanc, before we spent the rest of the day focusing on the movements of the dance in her luxurious lounge overlooking Kensington Square. We practised and practised, laughed and cried, spending hours trying to learn the difficult motion of the camel walk. Sadly she was never able to completely master it, but it certainly looked a bit better than when she began.

After that occasion, Joannie and I became great friends. I received many invites to her home, where we enjoyed the videos in the kasbah and finished the afternoons off by practising the dance to a piece of music that she was particularly fond of – 'The Spring' by Farid El-Atrache. She insisted I take a copy of the tape home and she neatly placed it in a cassette holder for me. Unfortunately, it was not a piece I could use for my venues as it was not suitable enough for my shows at the restaurant and I kept it tucked away amongst my other tapes.

We often chatted about the Chalayan, discussing at length my feelings towards Ata and his association towards me, and I found I began to rely on her reassurance about the relationship. He had put me on a pedestal, which I was naively relishing, enjoying the sense of magic that I was finding captivating and thrilling, but I needed her guidance and wisdom as to where it was heading and how long she thought the euphoric episode would last.

I invited her to the Chalayan to watch the show as she not only wanted to see me dance in public but she was intrigued to meet this charismatic man who had offered me such a wonderful opportunity by lifting me out of the dancing classes and making me a dancer in my own right. We both knew he was popular with the ladies, but who was this man who had changed my life?

That night she wore a beautiful white mohair stole around her shoulders and her hair neatly swept back behind her ears, showing off some pretty little diamond earrings that sparkled against her porcelain skin. She looked so beautiful.

Ata could not take his eyes off her, making sure she was comfortable and happy, offering her titbits from the menu and amusing her with his gregarious manner. He would not stop pampering her. She enjoyed every minute of it, accepting the attention and Ata's flattery. After my show, later that night, Ata and Pepe played the tambourine and drums wearing gigantic Mexican hats, and as Ata approached her, lifting his hat high above his head, he gently knelt on one knee, bowing his head and wooing her, asking her to accept his hand to dance. She was in her element as the customers roared with enthusiasm, goading them on. It was a wonderful evening and she took the stage that night.

It was a night we discussed more than once in fine detail but sadly, not long afterwards, I received a telephone call from her daughter to say her Mother had been admitted to Westminster Hospital after a major stroke. Then on the Sunday morning I got the devastating news that she had died that night. It was all so sudden and a terrible shock. She was only in her mid-fifties.

It was only then that I learnt she was Lady Joannie Hunt. She never told me, but it all made sense; the way she lived, the way she acted and the way she was.

A couple of months later, I decided to visit the Spiritualist church as I had heard that people were queuing to see Janet Smithers, a brilliant medium who I was familiar with, for a private sitting. To my amazement, she said she could see a lady shimmering in gold, laughing and saying 'it's all wobbly', and asked me if this made any sense. I remembered Joannie often danced in a gold costume and I believed it could be her. On my way home I remembered the tape she had given me on the first occasion I had visited her containing a piece of her favourite music I had not played because I felt it was not suitable for the restaurant. As soon as I got home, I rummaged through my belongings and was relieved to find it, still intact. As I opened the cassette, to my astonishment I found a £20 note wrapped around the tape, with a little letter inside, thanking me for all the patience I had given her that day in trying to help her learn the movement of the camel walk. My first thought was that I had never thanked her for her letter and gift, and for a moment a sense of guilt swept over me. When I put the tape on to reminisce, I could not believe what I was hearing because the music was all over the place. The tape was wobbly! It all made sense and after the tears, I took solace in the fact that her message had got through to me, and it was only then that I could eventually laugh in harmony with her.

*

Ingrid telephoned saying she had a booking for a temp with the Civil Service Treasury Solicitors in Waterloo Place overlooking the Mall. She did not know how long the booking was for, but could I go straight away?

Carlton House in Waterloo Place overlooks St James's Park with long terraces that encircle the building designed by John Nash. It is a beautiful pocket of London that is adorned with an abundance of statues and monuments. The most eye-catching is undoubtedly the Duke of York column, well-known for the nursery rhyme 'The Grand Old Duke of York' designed by Benjamin Dean Wyatt and stands at thirty-four metres tall, made of granite, and built between 1831 and 1834.

I was ushered into a salubrious office overlooking the terraces, just a step away from the heavy windows that guarded them in all their dignity and strength, composed to uphold in all weathers, overlooking the gardens of St James. The building gave a sense of power, achievement and pride, far beyond simple affluence in its structure, and was a refreshing change from some of the other solicitors' offices I had worked in.

There were two other secretaries in the room, not looking overworked, which is what you would expect in such a grand place, but acted like they had enough to keep them busy. One of the secretaries, Peter, was a young man, which I found unusual as 99% of secretarial staff were generally women, but he was an invigorating change from the norm with a great sense of humour and he kept both myself and the other female colleague entertained for most of the day.

I was happy there for a while apart from one solicitor, in his early forties with an army background, who sat at the end of the corridor with his door wide open, checking on everyone's movements as they passed by like a sergeant major. He was intent on noting down the times of employees' comings and goings, a pastime of his that gave him unauthorised authority which did not go down well with the rest of the staff. I felt I had to be doubly careful with times on my timesheet as I did not want to be caught arriving a few minutes late in the morning, having too many visits to the kitchen or leaving earlier than I should, as he was well known to cause friction amongst the employees working there.

He also had a tendency of regularly putting the word 'urgent' on his work so that he could jump the queue. It was a running joke amongst everyone in the office as the other solicitors remarked in disdain how often they were forced to put their work at the back of the queue because of his so-called 'urgent' work.

One day, I caught him in the kitchen making a cup of tea for himself and I explained my concern, with tongue in cheek, as to the stress he must be under with so much urgent work to get through. With a haughty air he explained that he was a very busy man, and that everyone was after him to get things done. As he was telling me his story, I was thinking that maybe he was wasting too much time checking on the timings of those around him rather than getting on with his work, but wisely kept the thought to myself as I did not want to cause friction. He had no sense of humour and gave me the impression that he was not happy in his work, whereupon I commiserated with him, explaining that I too had scruples about my job as a legal secretary but found that temping gave me varying challenges with new experiences, rather than being tied to a permanent position. He grunted as though he had nothing further to say but I took the courage to question him about why he was doing the job if he was not happy. He took his time to reply, stirring his tea, and eventually said, "Well, I get a good pension!"

Whilst working there during the daytime, I had an offer from a friend of Ata's who had seen me dance at the Chalayan and asked me to do a show at his large club in Birmingham as he was looking for something different to entertain his customers.

I agreed to do the show as he offered a good fee, including the cost of the train fare, and found it could be possible without staying the night as the last train from Birmingham to London was around 11.10pm, arriving in London for 1.15am, in time for a few hours' sleep before getting to work the next day.

I took my costume and other belongings in a holdall to the office, arriving at 9.30am, witnessing the solicitor jot down the time as I walked past, and at 5.30pm on the dot I left the office, which again was spotted by the same solicitor, to make my way to Euston Station. I caught the 6.30pm train, packed with commuters, taking approximately two hours to arrive at Birmingham New Street Station, where I queued for a taxi to take me to the club in the centre of town, which the driver knew well as it was a popular place for local punters.

The owner was pleased to see me and offered me something to eat and drink before getting ready for the show. It was a big place with plenty of mirrors on the walls, plush bright red seating and a large stage area. It seemed he knew Ata well, discussing him at length, and I felt he was sent as a spy to find out about my feelings towards him, which I was careful not to divulge as I did not want to give too much away.

The partygoers arrived in small droves and the atmosphere began to build. I was asked to get ready and was shown upstairs to a room where I could change. It was not until 10.05pm that a knock on the door informed me it was time to descend the stairs and wait for my cue. The show went well. I started on the stage but ventured towards the customers, where I stood on the chairs and tables and got people out to dance. They were a boisterous mixed crowd and the atmosphere was lively, but I managed to keep them entertained without mishap and I had a wonderful applause to acknowledge their thanks as I left the stage.

I knew I had little time to catch that last train back to London and the owner knocked on the door at 10.50pm to say that the taxi was waiting outside. On my leaving he gave me a handsome wad of notes for my trouble and once I got in the taxi, it was a race to get to the station so that I could catch that last 11.10pm train back to London. We did not have long and I noticed that with the traffic collecting in places, the minutes were ticking away. I paid my fare in haste as the driver said, "Hurry, run," which I did, through the large railway complex only to see the platform gates closing as I watched the back of the train slowly moving from the station on its way back to London. I had missed it! My heart fell to my shoes.

I did not want to return to the club and put the owner into the difficulty of having to accommodate me, which would have been embarrassing, especially as he would have been exhausted after a heavy night at the club, and I felt there was no point in trying to get a hotel room, which would have defeated the purpose of having gone there in the first place, and with only a couple of hours or so to kill before catching the 6.30am train back to London, I decided to find somewhere to sit in the station and pray that the hours would be kind to me. I easily found a seat in the empty station, but as it felt rather uncomfortable every so often, I invariably got up for a walk about to change the monotony, only to notice a middle-aged man strolling about the station who, like myself, had also just missed the last train. We cautiously smiled at one another, knowing we were the unlucky ones with the night ahead of us and little to do but wait until the early hours of the morning, so I thought I would be brave and say 'hello'. He seemed pleased I had made the effort and we started to talk. He was a pilot. He tested planes in the north of Scotland and needed to get back to see his family in London, who was expecting his arrival at any time. I smelt alcohol on his breath and came to understand he had visited a fellow colleague in Birmingham, stopping off before travelling onto London. He had an interesting career to which he was dedicated, but explained the difficulty he had in not having enough time to spend with his wife and family, which was causing problems. I sensed that all was not what it seemed at home and I queried whether missing the train at the last minute was a subconscious excuse to delay the reality of an unhappy marriage. He seemed to find solace in offloading with someone whom he had never met before and might never see again, and it helped both of us pass the time as I commiserated with him about his predicament.

The early hours eventually emerged as we knew they would, and at 6.30am we parted like two ships passing in the night as we lost each other looking for seats on a packed morning train, where I was relieved to close my eyes for an hour or two before arriving in London.

At Euston Station I had a quick wash in the ladies' and then made my way to Waterloo Place feeling absolutely shattered, but to my astonishment, I arrived at the office right on time at 9.30am on the dot and the nosy solicitor watching in the corridor had no idea of my overnight escapade or the difficulties I had experienced in trying to get to the office on time as he nonchalantly jotted down the time of my arrival.

I just tried to get through the day the best I could and oh, how glad I was to get home that evening at 7pm, crossing my fingers more than once that no one would call me, including Ata, who might have wanted to find out how my Birmingham trip went, ask me to do a show or pop round for a banter, as all I wanted to do was go straight to bed.

★

Soon afterwards Ingrid sent me out to work for Mr. Dominic Lee, the senior partner at a firm of Chinese solicitors in Soho, Chinatown, who specialised in conveyancing and could offer me flexible hours. He never kept an appointment diary as his clients, mainly shop owners and proprietors of Chinese restaurants, found it more convenient to just pop in at a moment's notice, which worked well for everyone.

Mr. Lee would often take me out for a Chinese lunch to meet some of his clients who owned the restaurants in the area, and we were often treated like king and queen as he was well respected within his community. I remember thinking how laid back he was from the usual solicitors I had worked for, not only because of his gentle manner but because he allowed me my own time-keeping, giving me the flexibility I needed.

I told Mr. Lee about my dancing and he asked me to organise a venue one night, so that he could bring some of his colleagues to watch me do a show.

I got in touch with Sheila, from my dancing class, who had just opened a restaurant with her Greek husband Harry down Rosebury Avenue in London called the Kolossi Grill, and she booked me in.

Sheila, a beautiful lady from Mauritius, with long black flowing hair danced well at the classes but did not want to perform in public, being a proprietor of her own restaurant and knowing I was dancing at the Chalayan and other places, asked me to do some shows for them when the opportunity arose.

There was always a jolly atmosphere there with Greek music playing in the background and as its location was in the centre of London, it was a perfect venue for Mr. Lee.

The date of the booking arrived but not until after one of the worst storms to hit the British Isles, for years. On the news bulletin they called it a 90 mile an hour hurricane that had caused havoc all over the country with many roads blocked by fallen trees, cancelled trains because of the debris on the lines and power cuts. Lincoln's Inn Fields had lost umpteen trees, as was the case with many of the parks in central London and scaffolding had collapsed from many of the buildings - creating chaos. I had been awake most of the night with the noise of the wind circling around my flat in Highgate and was not sure whether the buses would be running to get me to work the next morning as I heard on the radio that a lot of people had cancelled their engagements.

The news bulletins were asking the public to stay at home, and I was in a quandary whether to try and travel to work or not, as I could not contact either Mr. Lee or Sheila to know what they were doing. In my dilemma, I decided to pack my costume in any case and made my way down the road towards Parliament Hill Fields to see if any buses were running.

My hopes raised when I managed to get on a bus with others who also needed to get to work, but with many major roads cut off, I had to bus hop most of the journey which made it more hazardous than usual. When I finally got to work, to my surprise I found Mr. Lee was already there, sitting at his desk. He then told me that he was still eager to go that night with other colleagues who had managed to get into the office and after work we all clambered into a black taxi cab to take us to the restaurant. On our arrival Sheila and Harry warmly greeted us saying they were pleased we could make it as Rosebury Avenue had been closed off earlier in the day due to fallen trees on the road and that we were lucky to have missed all the problems as it had only just been cleared. Even though there had been so many difficulties because of the weather, with half of the country at a standstill, I was astonished to see the restaurant so busy and fully booked. It was as though nothing had happened.

Mr. Lee loved the show. I got him up to dance with me for a while and his colleagues were beaming from ear to ear as they watched on. It also went down well with the other customers and Sheila and Harry were terrific hosts. I was glad I had made the effort that day as apparently, Mr. Lee and his colleagues never stopped talking about it afterwards!

★

A couple of months later, I was offered another opportunity to work in a Turkish club called the Starlight, on Mare Street, Hackney, for six nights a week, with Sunday off. On that occasion the owner was a woman. She was an attractive Turkish lady, with a look of Britt Ekland, the Hollywood film star, admitting she wore a blonde wig. There was more of a relaxed feel about the club than the previous one I had attended, and I could mix with who I pleased without upsetting the hierarchy.

There was a small band occupying four musicians, playing similar instruments to where I had worked before, who stationed themselves at the back of the stage, with the layout more inviting than the previous club. They were friendly, spoke good English and often joined me for a chat in their breaks.

Candles, with their dim lighting, were placed on the tables, accompanied by large bowls of almonds wallowing in ice, which helped them expand to twice their size. This enabled the outer skin to peel easily before reaching the kernel inside. Customers in groups of five or six men or more would invite me to sit with them at their tables, which I always accepted, enjoying the banter, where they would take turns in offering me food on the end of cocktail sticks, something I had become accustomed to at other Turkish venues. There would always be one person in the group who thought he was the kingpin, instigating the chatter and jokes, whilst another in the group would sit quietly in the background. At the end of the evening, I was sometimes asked which one I had chosen as my favourite and, deliberately taking my time over the answer, I would eventually let them know that I preferred the quiet one, the one who looked shy, usually sitting at the end of the table. It was all light fun, there was nothing more in it, and my choice always caused a lot of laughter as the kingpin and all his entourage were expecting me to choose him, but I was never questioned about my decision!

There was no rigidity for the rota of the show as the owner, being a Turkish singer herself, chose when she wanted to perform on the stage, which suited me perfectly as I needed the flexibility, of being able to get from one place to another without worrying when I was going to dance.

I had been in the club over four months when one Saturday night, a beautiful young man sat next to me. There was an aesthetic air about him and he was noticeably stunning in his looks. His fine chiselled features were adorned with a mass of black shiny curly hair and he spoke perfect English. He told me he was a young student who wanted to do well in his life as a musician, having studied the oud, a very difficult instrument to play, and that he was hoping to get a job in one of the clubs. We talked for most of the night about our lives, when he admitted he was staying upstairs in the club on a makeshift bed as he had nowhere else to stay, but he was saving money and the situation suited him for the time being. On parting I wished him well, saying I might see him in a band one day and hoped to have the opportunity to dance for him at one of the venues. He smiled at my remark, but I never saw him again.

A couple of days later, on the Monday morning, I had a call from the police asking me my name and if I worked at the Starlight in Haringey as a belly dancer. Of course, I answered all the questions they asked me, but I was mystified as to why they had got in touch. The police sergeant then told me why he had phoned, giving me the shocking news that the club had been burnt down over the weekend, and said that he would appreciate my visiting the station to have a chat, which was not urgent, he said, but they needed to sort out their books.

I went along to the police station in Haringey the next day, explaining who I was, and at first they seemed confused as they were not expecting an English belly dancer to be working in a Turkish club, and they were even more baffled when they found out I was a legal secretary during the daytime. The sergeant asked me questions about the owner, who I said I did not know personally other than at the club, but that over the four months I had worked there I had been treated well by her. Then he told me the terrible news – that a young man was caught on fire on the first floor and had jumped from the window onto the pavement still alive, but sadly died later in hospital. Instantly I knew that it was that lovely young man as I remembered he had told me that he was staying in makeshift lodgings on the upper floors of the club; such a terribly sad story for someone who had such high hopes about succeeding in his life.

Months later, I happened to be working in a taverna in the same area, Ata Turk, when after I laid my veil down on the ground, a man from the audience came up onto the stage with a lighter and lit the veil to shreds. He was immediately hustled out in a brutish manner by the staff, never to be seen again, but I was told he used to be a frequent customer at the Starlight and obviously bore a revengeful streak about him. As far as I knew, the owner of the Starlight was not prosecuted for any misdemeanour to the property and was never charged as she had alibis to match her story. We never learnt what truly happened, other than that the young man's fatality was known to be an accidental death.

★

After a busy day in the office, queuing for buses and getting caught in long traffic jams, I often got home exhausted and frequently hoped I could have a quiet night in, but had agreed to be on call for parties at the Chalayan whenever I might be needed, so it was not always possible.

It was on such an evening arriving home, when I heard the phone ring to find it was Ata saying he had a party of people who wanted a dancer that night and would I come straight away? With little time to spare I made my way as soon as I could, knowing Ata had great ability to keep his customers amused and entertained before my arrival, and always had a bag ready containing everything I needed in case of such an emergency.

When I entered the restaurant on that occasion there was a loud cheer from the customers to greet me and to my amazement, I found that it was Ingrid from the agency, sitting with a large group of people waiting for my appearance. It was a big surprise as she had not told me she would be there with a large party, and Ata too was sworn to secrecy so that I would not know anything about it. The atmosphere was a buzz and Ata seemed pleased to see me, handing me a glass of wine as I walked in, and asked me to get ready as soon as I could.

This time he had brought his young son along with him and as I was changing in the dressing room he tapped on the door.

"It's Hussein. Can I come in?"

I always made sure I was respectable before allowing anyone to enter as I would have felt embarrassed otherwise, and as I had been given plenty of time to change, I let him in.

"Why have you put bright red lipstick on when you came in with maroon lipstick?" he asked seriously.

I did not have an answer, apart from explaining that I wore the maroon lipstick during the day and that I needed to change into a more vibrant colour to coincide with the costume I was wearing during the night. I avoided telling him that I needed to wear a more passionate colour for the show, which was not easy to explain to a little boy.

"Does it take a long time to sew the sequins?"

I replied, "Oh yes, each one has to be hand done!"

He was such an inquisitive, interested little boy, excitedly looking around at my costumes and asking me lots of questions.

"Why don't you put your hair up?" he asked.

I liked my hair on my shoulders, especially for the dance as it gave a gypsy appeal, but he insisted on seeing what it would look like on top of my head. As we practised various styles, we pulled faces at one another in the mirror, as I waited for him to agree with the style I preferred..

His little face looked on so intently, twisting his lip as he did, unsure if he liked it the way he had wanted it or whether to give in and let me have it the way I was finally going to wear it!

Then he said, "I expect the bra is very difficult to make."

I was a little taken aback, but yes, he was right! The bra had been very difficult to make and could be extremely uncomfortable to wear, particularly for long lengths of time. I was impressed with the observations of this young man who took such an interest in my garments with an unquenchable thirst for knowledge and boundless curiosity for everything around him. As I racked my brains to try and answer him in many instances, we often fell into fits of laughter about it all.

After a long hard day at work – and particularly after having worked in some of the clubs, where I saw a more serious side to the connection of the dance – I often found his company so refreshing with the light banter that we shared, the playfulness and the laughter that we had with one another, which never failed to put me in good spirits before a show.

Over the months and years of the many bookings that I had in Turkish and Greek restaurants and tavernas and many clubs, halls, weddings consisting of hundreds of guests, and even a Turkish factory, there was nowhere quite like the Chalayan. To me it felt very special. Ata was always attentive, the music was popular with a good mixture of songs that we all loved and knew from different countries, and there was a certain merriment about the place. The food was excellent, the customers were well looked after and there was always plenty of fun and humour amongst the staff. I felt part of the family. By the time I was to dance, with little Hussein having kept me company in the dressing room and both Ata and Pepe having created such a wonderful ambience, all I had to do was appear. I never missed a booking and I loved it there.

★

Ingrid sent me to a firm of litigation solicitors in the Temple. It was an area I had not visited for a long while since working there in Chambers as it had strong memories of my longstanding love affair with a senior barrister who later became a Judge in the middle of our relationship.

The solicitors, Bolton and Lowe, were past Fountain Court in the heart of Middle Temple. I entered through the double doors of the entrance and walked up the old oak staircase, which looked like it had been well used over the years, showing a dip in the centre of the stairs where everyone else had stepped previously. I climbed to the top floor where I was greeted by a pleasant receptionist who called for one of the secretaries to show me where to go. I was escorted into a bright airy room with windows all around, overlooking the wonderful view of the Inner Temple Gardens, and my desk was one of four as I was sharing with three other secretaries in the middle of the room.

It was a busy morning and to my surprise, later in the day, the senior partner asked us if we would like a glass of wine that we could have on our desks whilst working. Naturally, we all agreed, saying what a lovely idea it was, and we were told there was a reason behind the gesture as the Inner Temple was preparing for a summer party outside in the gardens and he did not want us to feel left out. It was such a nice thought and as we all looked out of the windows, we noticed small marquees already in place for the guests' arrival, surrounded by neatly dressed waiters and waitresses standing around, holding silver trays with glasses of champagne ready to hand out to anyone who approached them. It did not take long before a group of tail-coated young men started to walk towards the tables to grab the best seats, while a bevy of young ladies joined them, wearing hats and summer dresses, finding it difficult to walk on the grass in high heels. We could hear their laughter and jollity from a distance. As the party gained momentum, many guests began to accumulate in the grounds, but what made it special was the arrival of the Queen Mother, dressed in pale blue and topped with a powder blue feathered hat to match. She had a small entourage of distinguished men following her everywhere, making sure she was well looked after, and I watched her as she moved from one group to another, with her hat bobbing from side to side, showing she was intent on focusing on everyone personally. I could see from the window that she had a certain way about her, collecting her audience and keeping them amused as the guests began to swarm around her, adoring her, laughing with her, and showing a politeness that they probably did not share except on special occasions.

We forgot ourselves for a while as we watched the guests mingle on a lovely summer's day, enjoying themselves at the party outside in the gardens, and as we slowly sipped our wine, we too felt that we had been invited, almost forgetting that we were behind office windows.

I had to get back to work – there was so much to do – but with the staff in a merry mood and solicitors from other departments popping in most of the time to have a look at how things were evolving outside, it certainly took away the usual humdrum of an ordinary day's work, and I felt as though I had been paid to join in a social gathering rather than for my secretarial skills.

On my way home, towards Mitre Court, I walked past my old set of Chambers and all those old feelings I had for the man I once loved soon came flooding back. I took the opportunity to climb the quaint set of steps to the iron gate that led up to the Temple Church garden and I noticed many of the flowerbeds had changed and the ping pong ball mushroom had gone, but the magnolia was still there, even though not in flower. I could see through the window where my office once was, and was horrified to find it was filled with old cabinets, books and files. How sad it looked having no further use for anyone. It felt a long time ago. A tear fell onto my cheek as happy memories flooded back. I knew they had disappeared into the essence of time and I had to move away, accepting that one cannot return to the past.

★

Many times when dancing at places where I found that the atmosphere was lackluster, I made a point before the show of visualising myself at the Chalayan, with Ata announcing me, so that I could get that sparkle and enthusiasm I needed before a performance.

It was a policy I specifically needed when I got a little job at a swish restaurant called Sheikhs Tavern down Edgware Road, Marble Arch, London, which was beautifully adorned inside. Many varied lampshades of all different shapes and sizes hid the ceiling, with coloured tapestries covering the walls, while beautiful Arabic music played in the background. It was pricey. Not that many customers came in but when they did, it was the establishment's policy that I should dance when they arrived. The hierarchy was very strict, wanting me to stick to the hours whether it was busy or not, and it was against all principle to talk to the customers or converse with the waiters; this included not being allowed into the kitchen to meet the rest of the staff whilst I was waiting around before a show.

The atmosphere there was somewhat grim and impersonal, making it difficult to create an ambience, especially when there was no announcement or build-up for my entrance, or waiters to join or guide me towards the customers, and all I could do was just float around empty tables, returning to the group that had just sat down.

The most excruciating moment at the restaurant was early one evening when the place was empty, a lady came in on her own to order a dish from the menu. Whilst she was eating, I was told to get ready to do a show for her! I was being used as a masquerade rather than showing the reality of what I was trying to portray, and I felt it would have been better if I had been limited to a stage performance rather than trying to chivvy a woman on her own who seemed at a loss as to how to treat the situation.

I just appeared with no announcement and she looked up at me completely bemused, wondering what on earth I was doing dancing around her, occasionally tottering off now and again to include the other empty tables. She twitched away, not knowing what to do as she had no one with her to share her embarrassment, and I had to pretend that what I was doing was natural and expected of me. I tried to keep myself together for her sake as much as mine and I did not know who was more relieved when the show eventually came to an end. When I changed back into my normal clothes to sit on the settee until my next assignment, I noticed she had disappeared from the restaurant, not having stayed that long – and, it seemed, with the full intention of never returning again.

After three months of working there on a nightly basis, sometimes having to dance two or three times in an evening for the odd customers who drifted in, I soon lost interest in staying on and told them I had found somewhere else to dance and that I had to leave.

On my last evening there to cheer myself up, I decided to pop round to the Chalayan just to say 'hello'. I imagined it would be quiet as I had not heard from Ata over these last weeks, and hoped there would be a chance of seeing him there on his own, which was something I rarely did unless he contacted me first.

Whilst walking along the pavement towards the restaurant, there were a lot of late leaves on the ground, and as I strolled through them, I had a strong premonition that I would find some money amongst the foliage. I knew I would not be dancing and receiving tips that night but laughed to myself, believing in the possibility of finding some money amongst the thick layers of dead leaves that were lying on the ground and nonchalantly kicked them aside, mocking my premonition as I waded through them. Whilst doing so I kept a certain alertness, just in case. Then, to my utter astonishment, I believed I saw a different colour hue amongst the leaves. My heart skipped a beat with excitement as I bent down to pick up the wet mixture. I was completely dumbfounded to find it was a £20 note, wet and slimy from its unwanted exposure but gleaming in all its glory. A miraculous find. Then I wondered what was behind the message as it was the first time I was to visit the Chalayan without being invited, and looked upon the episode as a warning that my journey was important and comforted by the fact that my premonition in finding money was undoubtedly correct.

It was late. Ata was there and acknowledged my arrival straight away. "Elizabeth, what are you doing here?" he said with a big smile. I was hoping he would have been on his own and available to talk to as I needed to see him, but it was apparent he was entertaining and to my dismay, it looked as though he was accompanying a lady friend. He introduced me. "This is Maggie. She is from Scotland." She looked at me with wide eyes and a tiny smile. We had nothing to say to one another.

I went into the kitchen to waste a bit of time and Hassan the chef told me that she had been a friend of Ata's for a long time. I had no idea!

★

My goal was to work in a genuine Arab club as I wanted to experience the real thing with people who celebrated the authenticity of the dance and I put on weight deliberately as I was told Arabs prefer the larger lady to perform for them.

I had my eye on a club down Edgware Road and was waiting for the right time when I felt confident enough to approach them about a position as a dancer there.

The Aladdin was an Arabic club, with dancers and singers specially flown in from the Middle East. As I approached the doorway there was a bouncer barring me from entering and he asked me my name. I gave him my dancing name, Shariffa, and explained that I was looking for a job in the club, and he let me pass with a flick of the wrist.

The foyer was quite dark but swish. I could tell that money had been spent on the décor with the plush red carpet, fully enhanced by mirrors encircling the walls that could be intimidating if one did not want to look at oneself. A chandelier sparkled in the centre of the ceiling, slowly turning in a circular motion, and fresh flowers amassed around the skirting board. I made my way towards the spiral staircase, gingerly descending round and round to the lower floor.

Downstairs was a dining area, gloriously embellished with the same deep red carpet, with matching cushioned seats against beautifully laid tables ready for customers.

A simple stage was neatly placed in the centre of the dining room, empty but echoing what had been, what was and what could be, and while I tried to imagine myself appearing on that stage, I was interrupted by a tall, slender gentleman. He was wearing a pinstriped suit and eyeing me in a curious way, with a long moustache sitting cosily on his upper lip. I introduced myself and explained that I was wondering if there was an opportunity to work there as a dancer. He slightly bowed and with a smile, touching his chest by his heart, he told me his name was Mustafa. I acknowledged him, realising he did not know much English, but he kindly took me through to an alcove area where there was a bar and facilities to make tea. He muttered something to me about offering me a drink, and as I understood that Arabs might not approve of my sitting there with alcohol, I pointed to the tea urn, where he made me a cup of tea. Sadly though, there was no milk, so I had to make do.

I sat down at one of the tables by the bar and as time moved on, other Arabic men began to accumulate around the tables, talking in an erratic way. I noticed there was not much laughter shared between them as the chatter seemed to reach crescendos in heightened arguments. Some of them angrily pointed their fingers at one another, trying to emphasise that their side of the story was more important than the other. I just sat quietly sipping my tepid cup of tea whilst waiting patiently for someone to acknowledge me.

As the night wore on, more people arrived, mainly men, and the atmosphere became quite excitable and enigmatic. I lowered my eyes, avoiding the odd glance now and again as some of them were looking over at me, wondering who I was and why I was there.

Then the musicians arrived, a band of five who took their places on the stage. They chatted enthusiastically with one another whilst tuning their instruments, before playing a beautiful piece of Arabic music, changing the atmosphere and filling everyone's hearts with hope. A very large man entered the arena, taking his place at one of the tables, almost occupying two seats because of his size, and all the surrounding chatter suddenly ceased. Everyone ran around him, asking if he wanted anything, looking after him and offering him tea. He waved them away and started playing with his worry beads between his fingers as he gradually closed his eyes, allowing the music to wash over him. Mustafa came over to me. "The owner, the owner," he repeated, which did not surprise me, considering the attention he had been receiving. But I did not feel it was the right time to introduce myself just at that moment. I waited for the band to take a break before I took the courage to approach him and ask him if there was a vacancy as a dancer at his club when he looked at me as though half asleep.

"Did you bring costume?" he asked in a light, soft voice. I replied that I had. He nodded, saying, "OK." He was obviously a man of few words as nothing more was said between us and I felt I had to return to the table where I had been sitting. One of the band members came over to me, introducing himself as Yasin from Egypt. He spoke reasonable English and as I explained I was there hoping to get a job as a dancer, he told me to hold on and keep waiting around, as the owner could ask me to dance at any time during the night.

I waited patiently until the early hours of the morning for something to happen, with everyone sitting around drinking tea. Occasionally, a member of staff would sit with me to keep me company for a while but as we did not speak the same language it was a little difficult to communicate. As the night wore on, I was beginning to think I had been forgotten, when suddenly Mustafa tapped me on the shoulder, saying eagerly, "Change, change." A sudden rush of nerves overwhelmed me for a moment, and I began to wonder what I was doing there. Mustafa took me to a little room at the back of the premises where I could change saying, "Music, music." He wanted to know the piece of music I had chosen for the band to play. I replied saying 'Azziza', or a piece played for Fifi Abdul or Nagoua Fouad, famous belly dancers in Egypt, and with a smile he ran off.

The ceiling was low and shaped like an arch and the room was filled with old carpets and broken instruments, which looked as though they had been dumped for a while with nowhere else to go. There was a strong smell of incense that had steadily accumulated since there was no air vent or window. I tried not to dwell on the surroundings as I did not know how long they would give me to change and decided to just get on with it. After a while, there was a tap on the door. It was Mustafa, asking if I was ready. I opened the door with difficulty whilst wearing my finger cymbals and at the same time trying to hold a veil around me. Mustafa smiled quickly before leaving me there, and I waited until I eventually heard my music 'Azziza' begin. It was my cue to approach the stage. The music has a long start, which gave me plenty of time to leave the dressing room, walk through the bar area and glide through the restaurant to arrive on the stage in time.

Some customers had arrived, filling a few of the tables, but being a Monday night it was not that busy, which I was relieved about as it was my first opportunity practising with the band. I focused on the stage and kept up with the music, finishing with a small drum solo, shimmer and spin, and as I returned to the dressing room, everyone in the bar area smiled at me as I ran through, although I could not see the owner.

After I had changed and left the dressing room, Mustafa explained that the owner wanted to see me and led me into a little back room where I found him sitting next to a lady who spoke reasonable English. "What is your name?" she asked. I gave her my Christian name and dancing name. Her dark eyes penetrated through mine with no expression or warmth and her voice sounded sharp, like a knife cutting through the air as she spoke. Her partner, the owner, just leant back in his chair, clutching his worry beads, allowing her to do all the talking. "You have lessons, yes?" she said. "Then you come back here, yes?" I did not really understand what she meant, but she got up to open the office door to call for a lady called Zeta, who came in looking agitated, glancing over in my direction. "You teach this lady, OK?" she said to Zeta, who I could see was not too happy about her new role but nevertheless agreed reluctantly to what had been asked of her and, with a fair amount of confusion, we left the room.

After Selwa's classes and all the shows that I had done, I did not feel I had much more to learn, but it seemed I had no choice in the matter and therefore went along with the status quo, which meant I was somewhat vulnerable in Zeta's hands.

"I'm to show you the process of the dance," Zeta said. "It will cost you £50. You only need one lesson." I thought it was my only chance, so I agreed to her price. Then she openly told me she was looking for a job there, saying she had worked at the club before but had been in Egypt for three months and now wanted to return. I understood her dilemma and disappointment, explaining that I was not happy about what had happened but that I just wanted the experience of working in an Arab club. She emphasised that it was not my fault and she did not blame me, but that the owners had not kept their promise to re-employ her and it had upset her. I could see her point of view as I would have been devastated if Ata had replaced me with a new dancer, especially if he asked me to train the new dancer to take my place. On the other hand, I did not feel she had a personal connection with the owners in the same way that I felt I had with the Chalayan, and being a club, variety was needed every now and again for the customers. I lifted her hopes with the fact that I believed she probably would retrieve her position there in time after a change of performers, and we parted swapping telephone numbers, agreeing to meet the next day.

There was not a lot of space in her lounge and I could tell she was not prone to giving lessons, but told me what I needed to know and how to look more professional in the way of protocol with the band and the customers. She explained to me that the dancer was the conductor of the band and able to lead now and again rather than follow, as I had done to a certain extent during my audition. I was to understand that the music would be played right through, without variation, unlike the procedure at Turkish venues where the music lingered for the dancer to work for tips. The whole piece of music was to be well choreographed and practised never leaving the stage. The veil was of great importance in that when it was released in a certain section of the music, it was to signify that the dancer had let go of her virginity.

Zeta showed me how to concentrate on and dance to a different instrument within the same piece of music. She explained that the musician whom I had chosen would automatically be aware of my choice through my movements and follow the flow. There were various drum solos, eight or more rhythms, which a dancer should learn off by heart and, at an appropriate time in the music, call out the name of the solo of her choice, which the drummer would demonstrate for her. It was a partnership that had to be timed and practised to perfection.

Arabic drummers are trained in college from an early age to master the skill. She explained that an Arabic dancer never – and repeated the word 'never' – approaches customers to beg for tips; that they are to remain on the stage throughout the performance. A customer, if he so wishes, will approach the dancer on the stage and pour money in note form above the dancer's head, allowing it to float to the ground. There is no touching between the customer and the dancer. She said never to bend down to retrieve money from the floor; money would be collected from the stage by well-trusted staff who would distribute a third to the band and a third to the owner, leaving the final third for the dancer.

Finger cymbals were used for a specific section in the music if so wished, but then removed and placed on the stage afterwards, and not used to entice customers or played during the rest of the performance I realised, after spending time with Zeta, where I had shown my naivety of Arabic traditions and hoped that after her influence, I had learnt enough to help get me the job.

★

I had been at the Chalayan for about five years. It was a Saturday and Ata appeared to be in a particularly happy mood that evening as I carried out the show to a packed audience, feeling it was a necessary hors d'oeuvre in preparation for my second audition at the Aladdin later that evening. After the show Ata brushed passed me in the dressing room to change the music, and whilst he was choosing a tape, I could sense he wanted to talk to me personally, when he uttered the words that I dreaded to hear – that he was to marry Maggie, the Scottish lady, on New Year's Day.

I could not believe what I had heard. I was dumbfounded. Even though I already knew about Maggie and was aware that she was a friend of his, I had no idea he had such a strong attachment for her in that way. It was a bombshell and completely unexpected.

Realising I had to get to the Aladdin for an important audition, I gathered my belongings in a hurried fashion and walked past the customers with a stony expression on my face. Even though they called my name and tried to catch my eye to stop me for a quick chat, I left in haste without saying goodbye to anyone.

★

I arrived at the Aladdin to a busy, vibrant atmosphere, it being a Saturday night, with quite a few customers already seated at the tables, and was informed that a singer had been especially flown in from Egypt to end the show.

I knew I had to hide Elizabeth and focus on Shariffa. I could not let my emotions take over and let the opportunity go. Over the few years I had been dancing, I learnt how to act and forget who I was, and this was one of those occasions.

The owner had taken his place amongst the tables, clutching his worry beads. I was to be the first on and I was asked to get ready by a member of the band.

I heard my music begin and slowly glided towards the stage, swirling my veil to the melody of the music. As I encircled the stage with strong hip movements, allowing the veil to play around me, I started to lower it at the appropriate moment when the music changed. Then I continued dancing with soft gentle movements to the taksim as I let the veil gradually fall to the floor. A member of staff ran onto the stage to remove it for safety reasons, and the drum beat began to play a hypnotic rhythm, revving the music to a higher scale. It was time for the dancer to smile and show her confidence after the solemnity of the dropping of the veil, and revel in a sense of freedom. I chose to follow the drum throughout on this first occasion as it was the simplest instrument to portray, focusing on its rhythmic beat. Yasin shouted his support in Arabic and I knew I was synchronising with the band. I disciplined myself to stay on the stage throughout the show and when it was time to call out for my drum solo, Beledi, which was used by most dancers, there was another shout from a member of the band acknowledging his approval. I finished with a full thrust shimmer as the musicians followed my movements into a small spin, and as I bowed to end the show a customer came running up onto the stage, dropping a handful of notes on top of my head, which slowly filtered to the ground, and another cheer echoed behind me as I left the stage.

After I had changed, Mustafa came up to me. "Office, office," he said, pointing me to the door of the little back room. I entered and recognised the same lady I had seen before sitting next to the owner, who was concentrating on twiddling his worry beads.

"You work here, yes?" the lady said, flashing her familiar black eyes.

"Yes," I replied. My heart was thumping with excitement.

"You arrive at 11.30pm or midnight, and you start the show at 2am. You leave not before 6.30am. OK? Six nights a week, starting next Monday, OK?" I nodded in agreement.

"If customers want you to sit at their table, it is an honour, OK? And if they offer you a drink, you ask for champagne."

I explained in the best way I could that I did not mind sitting with the customers on occasion, but that I wished not to show interest in them otherwise. The owner suddenly wagged his finger as though to say no, that was not necessary, and the lady agreed that as far as they were concerned, they did not entertain any business connection outside the club. She changed the subject abruptly, offering me a reasonable sum of money to be paid each week, adding that my third of the tips would be given to me at the end of the week. It sounded a good salary even though I had no idea how much to ask for, and was quite happy to accept what was offered as I always had my secretarial skills to fall back on if there was any shortfall or if I needed emergency funds.

I left the office absolutely thrilled, knowing that I had accomplished something that I had always wanted to do, and sat with other members of the staff to watch the rest of the show for the remainder of the evening. There was a surge of excitement erupting as one of the singers from Egypt had just taken the stage.

After the singer's performance, there were two other dancers from the middle east and I hoped I would sense that magic that inspired me a few years before in Morocco, but sadly it was not to be. I do not know if it was because I had witnessed Selwa's magnificent dancing, both in the classes and on the stage, or because I had progressed myself to a certain level or because I had become too familiar with the movements, but I just felt a certain disappointment about their performances.

Later, when I learnt that one of the dancers had been paid £10,000 by a customer to stay with him for a couple of nights, I realised that perhaps she was not too interested in perfecting the art of the dance, but used that line of work to be more involved in other pursuits, which made me aware once again of the vulnerable circumstances a dancer could place herself in. But I began to understand that there were two types of dancers: those who wanted to perfect the dance for its own sake, and those that used the dance for other purposes – both of which had a place in a club.

When the final singer, a prima donna from Egypt, came onto the stage to start her repertoire, she brought the place down. The whole club heaved with the blend of music as she rhythmically cascaded from one aria to another. She was unbelievable. Her costume glittered under the lights as she dabbed her forehead occasionally with a napkin that was constantly replaced for her by an adoring fan. She had a certain confidence about her, a strength one could not pinpoint, and I found her fascinating to watch. The music was superb and as I was sitting there, I felt very fortunate to be allowed to witness such a spectacle and stayed on to watch the whole show to the end.

Leaving at 6.30am in daylight and catching a bus from Marble Arch back home to Highgate, I noticed I was travelling in the opposite direction from the flow of the daily commuters coming into London to start a day's work. As I looked out of the window of the bus, I could see an image of my reflection in the pane of glass and remembered who I was – Elizabeth, slowly emerging, as she does, with the presence of Shariffa silently slipping away into the distance. As the process took place, so did the awareness of the news of Ata's marriage, open and raw, gradually and painfully start to dawn on me.

★

It was New Year's Eve and I had to return to the Chalayan to collect a costume that I had left behind the night before. I decided to pop up there in the daytime, hoping it would be empty with no one about, but to my dismay I found Ata with his family, sitting around the tables discussing their future. I felt very out of place as Ata's fiancée was also there and I apologised for my intrusion. Ata insisted that I sat down to join them, which I did not really want to do, and Hussein noticing my discomfort went into the kitchen to get me a cup of tea. It was not an easy moment as Ata was talking about selling the restaurant and opening a place in Plymouth.

I heard Hussein ask his father if I could come too, to which Ata replied, "Yes, of course, she will be invited as a special guest." But it was not really what I wanted to hear as I had no intention of travelling all the way down to Plymouth with being nothing more than a special guest when I already had a very busy schedule in London.

I told everybody that I could not stay as I had a lot of shows that evening, being New Year's Eve, and that I was in a bit of a rush. On my way out, Ata shouted after me, "See you tonight." He wanted to make sure that I would arrive on time as he had a lot of parties booked for the evening and needed me to arrive before the sound of the midnight chimes of Big Ben so I could bring in the new year as I had done for many years previously. I left, reassuring him that I would be there in good time to do the show, and Hussein followed me out into the street. He could ssee I was upset and I was very touched by his concern as I tried to make conversation with him and put a smile on my face, but we both knew I was trying to hide my true feelings.

*

My first venue was early evening at the Kantara in Covent Garden. I danced upstairs for customers sitting at tables, who were mainly the general public and tourists. They were lively and enjoying the beginning stages of the New Year festivities, generally enjoying the fun of it all and acknowledging their goodwill by placing plenty of notes in my costume.

Afterwards I went down to the basement where I danced for a noisy office party who were throwing poppers and streamers all over the place. Unscathed, I left on time and managed to hail a black cab to take me to my next venue – a Turkish restaurant, Efes, in Oxford Circus. There I danced to a packed audience with a live band. I stood on the tables and made a lot of tips. The owners paid me on time so that I did not have to wait around, which was appreciated, and left a lot of happy people who wanted me to stay, which I would have loved to have done under different circumstances but I had to get to Kolossi Grill, where Sheila and Harry were waiting for me.

The Kolossi Grill often had some interesting customers from around the area as groups of journalists from popular newspaper offices close by would book tables mid-week. They were a lively crowd, not short of conversation or afraid of spending their money and always gave good reviews of the restaurant in their magazines and newspapers.

The restaurant was also frequently fully booked by the police force, who had a local station in the vicinity, to celebrate their parties. They were a friendly mixed bunch when they were not on duty, from different departments of the police, and when I told them that I was a legal secretary during the day, they rolled around with laughter, sharing jokes like naughty – but nice - schoolboys!

On this occasion, I danced for a heavy crowd of office goers from an accountants' office, wearing Christmas hats and throwing streamers, poppers and balloons in every direction, with the party in full swing before my arrival I managed to entertain them by using a lot of comedy in my show, playing around with some of the customers, standing on the tables and swopping the Christmas hats they were wearing by placing them on different heads, and generally having fun with them. The show went well, and they cheered me as I left to make my way to the Chalayan. There was a taxi waiting outside already paid for by Sheila as she knew I would have had great difficulty in hailing an empty black cab late on New Year's Eve to get to Ata's before midnight. I blew kisses to her from the back window in thanks of her generosity.

I mentioned to the driver that I had to arrive at the Chalayan before midnight, which was paramount, but whilst I was there could he wait for me to take me to Marble Arch afterwards for my performance at the Aladdin. He was happy with that arrangement and did his best to get me to Ata's by taking shortcuts through the streets of London as the roads were getting heavier with traffic. With revelry heightening amongst groups of people who sometimes strolled onto the roads in front of the cars to get to where they wanted to go, I bit my nails at the back of the cab, hoping we would get there on time. The clock carried on ticking closer towards the hour as the driver weaved through the traffic with skill and it was such a relief to finally arrive at the doors of the Chalayan for 11.50pm, giving me that precious ten minutes before the show at midnight.

The place was buzzing with excitement. I was already high on adrenaline. The party was swinging with Ata at his best and Hussein was there, telling his father that I looked like Kate Bush, which was a much needed boost to my confidence. I reciprocated, saying he looked like Elvis Presley, twisting his lip as he did, whereupon we laughed together, but his father indicated that he wanted me to hurry up and get ready, showing that he did not have time for personal chatter.

With all the hypertension connected to the occasion, it was also the show I dreaded the most as I was unsure as to whether it could be my last at the Chalayan, for the next day – New Year's Day – Ata would be a married man. But it was not the time to dwell on such matters as I had a show to do.

Whilst I got ready in the dressing room, Ata came in. He kissed me on the lips for a very long time. "That is from the heart," he said, "from the heart." He left the room with what I thought was a tear in his eye. My music began just seconds after the midnight gongs, all beautifully timed, and I was joined by both Ata and Pepe playing the drums and tambourines as always to an animated audience, bringing the place down.

★

After the marriage ceremony, Ata went away on a long holiday with his new bride, which gave breathing space between us, and I was left to consider my future and contemplate whether I wanted to leave or remain dancing at the restaurant as it appeared the choice was up to me.

Hussein was fifteen, reaching sixteen, years of age when his father remarried and he went over to Cyprus to stay with his own mother for a while. That is when we lost contact. I knew that on his return to the UK, he would have a new stepmother to befriend and I felt it was time for me to detach myself from the family, as I was satisfied with the knowledge that he was doing well in his studies and excelling at school. He had his whole life ahead of him and all I hoped was that he would find that niche he was looking for in the world, that he should be successful and that he could aspire to the heights he wanted to achieve. But most of all, I wanted him to be happy.

In the meantime, Ingrid sent me out to a firm of solicitors. It was only a one-day booking at the beginning of the year, which I accepted as there was a lull after the Christmas rush of shows and, rather than dwelling on things at home, I needed to be occupied, even though it meant working in a solicitors' office.

The firm was the other side of London Bridge and as it was a blustery, wintery day, I tried to keep my balance in the wind as I walked along the pavement to reach the other side. The Thames looked grey and choppy, deep and cold, and I thought how uninviting it appeared, especially as I could not swim, and wondered how I would save myself if I happened to topple over into the waters below.

The office was nothing special and it was quiet most of the morning. Then at midday an old employee returned after having been away for the Christmas break and everyone in the office suddenly rose from their desks to greet her, singing, "Here comes the bride, here comes the bride," as apparently she had just returned from her honeymoon!

★

Over the coming weeks and months, Ata's appearance at the restaurant decreased substantially with Saturday being the only busy night, when he would usually pop in to help Pepe with the show, and as I decided to carry on dancing at the restaurant whilst he was considering his future there, I deliberately left earlier than usual, not hanging around to join in the chatter with everyone afterwards as I had done in the past.

A Turkish restaurant/club called Barbaros, down Lordship Lane, offered me a job as a dancer, working for them six nights a week. The club had just opened and Abraham, the owner, phoned to say he needed my attendance at a photoshoot, with a small band of three, to advertise the date of their opening for a Turkish magazine, *Novotel*.

The club became very popular, particularly on Saturday nights, which I was able to attend after the Chalayan, and my show had been arranged to take place between the two Turkish singers. When I heard the first singer begin his second song, it was my cue to get ready in a little dressing room behind the kitchen, where I waited until I heard my announcement. The show would last between twenty minutes to half an hour depending on the audience, and because the club was always busy on a Saturday night, I took two costumes with me in case I was needed to dance again later in the early hours of the morning.

A couple of doors down the road, a new Greek club, Aphrodite, had also just opened, with expensive cars parked outside. As the venues were not in competition with one another, catering for different cultures, I recognised the benefit of their proximity and after my show at the Barbaros one night, I went to talk to them about dancing there. They were very welcoming, and when they learnt that I was dancing next door for the Turkish club, they showed an interest and offered me a spot between the singers in the very early hours of the morning.

I had already experienced working with Greek musicians in restaurants and clubs over the years as they enjoyed the entertainment of a belly dancer at their venues, although I often found the bouzouki a very difficult instrument when practising the traditional aspects of the storytelling of the dance. But as the show was on a different format to the Arabic and Turkish shows I was able to ad lib and change the tempo where necessary to suit the venue. There was a strong family feel there, with guests ranging from the old to the young, sharing tables with their friends and neighbours who all joined in to enjoy each other's company, and I was always assisted up onto the tables by pleasing customers who would place good tips in my costume.

After the show, before I left, I always made a point of acknowledging the band by sharing a portion of my tips with them, who openly showed their appreciation for my contribution by cheering me as I left the premises.

★

*Photoshoot for Turkish magazine 'Novotel'*
*with band and Abraham at The Barbaros Taverna*

*Chris Michael's pix for audition*

*Chris Michael's pix for audition*

*Chris Michael's pix for audition*

*My audition at the Chalayan*

*John Mowlem Plc 'Top Out' on the Natwest Tower rooftop*

*Eddie George, Governor of the Bank of England,*
*making a speech at Natwest Tower 'Top Out'*

Nigel Barker, Document Controller in portacabin at the Guildhall

*Ray Cutts, Project Manager of Mowlems with dignatories at the new Art Annex, Guildhall East Wing*

*Press and media at the Guildhall 'Topping Out*

*(L) Picture of my Mother Joan M.Davies MFPS*
*(R) www.PlonkStory.com*

*Outside Palais des Beaux Arts, Paris*
*Hussein Chalayan MBE Fashion show*
*'Pasatiempo' with 'Plonk' clothes*

# MY TRIP TO CYPRUS
## SUMMER MONTHS

After six months or so working at the Barbaros, the owners – Abraham and his brother Erol – wanted to close the club over the early summer months to visit their mother and the rest of the family in Northern Cyprus, and invited me to join them for a free holiday. I needed a change and as it seemed an offer too good to miss and accepted joining them for a fortnight's break.

Many years before, in 1970, I had visited the Greek side of the island with my mother and brother on a Mediterranean cruise to Beirut – besides stopping at two beautiful islands, Rhodes and Crete, on the way – and we disembarked at Limassol in Cyprus. A young Greek Cypriot barrister, completing his pupillage in Chambers in London, offered to meet us and take us around the island by car. It was hot, with stunning views. We stopped off at British Army barracks, as they were noticeably prevalent around the island, and our photos were taken standing next to soldiers who appeared used to the practice, deliberately smiling into the camera as though it was part of their job.

On this holiday, I was to visit the northern Turkish side of Cyprus to meet the brothers' mother and the rest of the family, who lived in a villa high up in the mountains, which they said they had built themselves in the Tilliria region. As I could take a friend with me, I introduced them to Helen from the dancing classes, and a few weeks later we were on our way to Cyprus.

As there were no direct flights to Northern Cyprus, we had to change at Antalya Airport to carry on with our journey, but when we landed we were told that the airline had overbooked our flight to Cyprus and that there were no connecting flights for a week. We were horrified to learn that we would have to wait for that length of time, but they consoled us by laying on a coach to take us on a ten-hour trip to Adana Airport overnight, where it was expected we could catch a connecting flight to Cyprus the next morning.

Helen and I sat on the back seat of the coach, believing we would have more room by being able to put our legs up, but after a while we found it extremely uncomfortable as the coach constantly jumped around on uneven ground, making it impossible to sleep. To make matters worse, the coach kept breaking down and even though the driver was a good mechanic, he relied on the assistance of other drivers who would stop to help so that we could get back on our journey. Without their mechanical skills, I doubt we would ever have arrived at the airport on time. After being buffeted about all night on the back seat, with dawn eventually breaking we miraculously arrived at Adana Airport, where we joined long queues at passport control to finally board the plane to Cyprus, which was such a welcome relief.

After a long and gruelling journey, we felt like wet rags when we finally arrived at the airport in Larnaca, Northern Cyprus, but we were able to organise a taxi to take us to Yesilirmak, way up in the mountains, where the brothers lived with their mother and father and the rest of their family. When I was a child, I always thought what a brilliant driver my father was, with such a cool nerve as he dealt with the hairpin bends in the south of France on our way to Monte Carlo. This was just as treacherous, if not more, with the twists and turns in the road travelling high up into some of the most difficult terrain. After one set of hairpin bends there was another, with no apparent reprieve, making our ears pop as we drove high up into the mountains. One false move would have cost us our lives, but the taxi driver seemingly did not have a care in the world, casually chatting and laughing as though the whole experience was second nature to him. Many a time we held our breath in the back of the car, praying not to see another car free-wheeling downhill from the opposite direction.

The views were impressive for miles around, as though flying in an aeroplane looking down at the layers of rock formation with the abundance of foliage and forests surrounding the area underneath, and it was a welcome sight to see a gleaming white villa ahead of us as the driver acknowledged we had arrived at our location.

Erol and Abraham were waiting for us, waving, acknowledging our arrival, and immediately took our bags from the boot of the taxi. A little old lady, the brothers' mother, dressed from head to toe in a long shawl, greeted us with such a lovely smile.

We were shown to our rooms and to our delight found we had a little flat all to ourselves, with our own personal lounge and TV, and even a small kitchenette laid on. Our lodgings were far more than we expected and such a wonderful surprise after our long journey. Helen had a shower straight away then she lay down on the clean sheets of her newly laid bed and slept like a baby for twelve hours.

We were both feeling much more refreshed the next morning and after breakfast with the family, one of the brothers drove us down the hairpin bends to an awaiting sandy beach below. It was like paradise. There was a small taverna on the corner where we could get ice creams and cold drinks and we stayed there most of the day, enjoying the white sand, sea and palm trees. Later in the afternoon, one of the brothers came to collect us to take us back to the villa, where members of the family had spent most of the day preparing combinations of different mezes as I had grown to know at the Chalayan, all laid out on a large wooden table outside on the patio.

As the night set in, we heard the pleasant sound of the cicadas on the trees, and as we got together around the table, it gave us a chance to get to know the family and discuss our lives. Afterwards we sang songs to Turkish Cypriot music, dancing around the tables and drinking plenty of wine till very late in the evening.

On the days we did not go down to the beach, the brothers introduced us to a friend of theirs, Atilla, who worked for the Water Board and whose job it was to sort out the difficulty that the Turkish Cypriots were still having in receiving drinking water because of Greek restrictions from their side of the island, which had been a continuing problem since the invasion in 1974.

He told us some horrific stories about the Greek military junta who in December 1963 started to ruthlessly attack Turkish Cypriots across the island in small towns and villages, witnessing bodies unceremoniously left at the side of the road. In 1964, Lieutenant General George Karayiannis referred to the Ethnikos plan as the blueprint for the annihilation of the Turkish Cypriots to create the union of Cyprus with Greece. On 28th December 1963 the Daily Express carried the following report from Cyprus.

> "We went tonight into the sealed-off Turkish Cypriot quarter of Nicosia in which 200 to 300 people had been slaughtered in the last five days. We were the first Western reporters there and we have seen sights too frightful to be described in print. Horror so extreme that the people seemed stunned beyond tears".

It was known that the invasion of a wealthy Greek holiday resort – Varosha, near Famagusta – by the Turks years later in 1974 was revenge for the massacres by the Greek junta. Although not a shot was fired, and neither was there death nor injury from the invasion, it forced the Greek residents to flee from their homes with their lives and to this day it remains a ghost town with the UN blocking entry as protectors.

Atilla was quite emotional about telling his side of the story, but as he wanted us to have a good holiday he carried on driving us around to visit different parts of the island, where we were able to explore some of the heritage. We visited the Soli ruins, dating back to the sixth century BC – once an ancient Greek city but since 1974, part of the Turkish Republic of Northern Cyprus. What remains today is mainly from the Roman period. It is most notable for the wonderful mosaic floor of the basilica, which shows off a wealth of birds, animals and geometric designs. Still recognisable and most outstanding of all is the byzantine swan mosaic in the middle of the structural foundation.

Afterwards, we visited Vouni, a picturesque village with cobbled alleyways, and traditional houses with wooden doors and large windows, narrow balconies and inside yards. It was an unforgettable hamlet to visit. Being hot, dusty work, travelling in the heat to those places, it was such a relief to stop at a little taverna and enjoy cold drinks. Vouni Palace is above sea level on a cliff top, thought to have been built during the Persian occupation in the fifth century BC. Later it was found that the foundations were destroyed by the Soli inhabitants.

We finished our trip with the birthplace of Aphrodite of Soloi – Kouklia in the Aphrodite Hills near Paphos – an ancient Greek goddess born from the foam of the sea, associated with love, beauty, passion, sexuality and procreation. What more could a man want! Apparently, she had a belt that had the power to cause others to fall in love with the wearer. She had many lovers but married Hephaestus, who was not seen as a threat because of his ugliness and deformity, but her true love was Ares, the god of war. Aphrodite and Ares were known to be the parents of Eros and Anteros.

Visiting all these places stretches the mind with the knowledge that man lived long before one's own existence, and one cannot help but admire some of the wonderful architecture that they left behind.

During our stay, Atilla also drove us to Kyrenia with its famous harbour, incorporating the shipwreck museum with its collection of ancient artefacts, and then we visited a sixteenth-century castle built by Venetians where a twelfth-century chapel lies within its walls.

Afterwards, he took us all the way to Nicosia – or Lefkosia, as it is officially known – the capital of the island, with its curious and fascinating mix of vibrant street life, shops and restaurants, where we stopped to enjoy something to eat and drink before the long drive back to the brothers' villa in Yesirilirmak.

On the last night of our holiday, the brothers treated their family, friends and neighbours, and Helen and I, to a visit to one of the largest local tavernas on the island with live music, excellent food and plenty of dancing. We all had a great time and before we left, the owner, Ibrahim, happily gave us his telephone number in case we ever wanted to return one day.

It was a wonderful holiday, basking on the beach, enjoying the kind hospitality of the people and visiting the beautiful sights of Cyprus, and I felt somewhat emotional when I said goodbye to the brothers' mother, who had put so much effort into looking after us over the holiday, and I had that strange feeling – as one does on occasion – that I would never see her again.

After returning to London, the two brothers decided to close the club, which was not a surprise as their lease was about to expire and they were not looking at renewing it. I had been dancing there for over six months, with the holiday thrown in, and I accepted that change was inevitable after having enjoyed my time with them.

I did not keep track of the brothers' movements afterwards or find out what happened to them, or whether they had opened another taverna or a Turkish restaurant somewhere else, but I believe one of them remarried, returning to his family in his beloved Cyprus, leaving his brother in the UK to fend for himself.

★

On my return from Cyprus, Ata introduced me to the new owner, Ali, from Istanbul, who said he would like to keep me on as a dancer there and hoped that I would agree as the rest of the staff – Pepe, Hassan the chef and Mary – had already accepted to remain in their present jobs. It was not an easy decision at first as I had been considering severing myself from the restaurant once Ata left, but on the other hand, as I had been there so many years, getting on well with the staff and a lot of the customers, I looked upon it as a consolation prize and accepted Ali's offer.

He kept the same name, Chalayan, and as he decided not to redecorate, the place kept its original appeal. Ali was in his early fifties, looking older than his years with a head of white hair, married with two young sons and eager to carry on the business as it was. He was a reasonable man who paid me well, keeping me busy, especially on Saturday nights and with a few parties thrown in during the week, we worked well together. But Ali was not Ata, and as the days went by I felt that the heart had been ripped out of the place; that vibrancy, that euphoric hold that I once felt so attached to had gone, and as much as I enjoyed dancing there, it never really felt quite the same.

It had only been four weeks or so since my holiday to Cyprus, and as I was not too happy in my temp secretarial post working for a firm of solicitors called Nabarro & Co., in Piccadilly, I knew I had to do something crucial about my predicament. So during my lunch hour I decided to phone Ibrahim, the Turkish Cypriot I had met in Cyprus, and told him that I would like to work as a dancer for a couple of months in his taverna in Famagusta. He seemed very surprised at first, but then said he could organise board and lodging for me and that if I danced free of charge, I could keep all the tips I might earn.

Ali accepted the break as he too was going on holiday to

Istanbul with his family at the same time, closing the Chalayan for the summer months, and told me my job was open for me on my return.

So, I packed my bags.

★

How I got all my costumes and other clothes into the two small suitcases that I had, I will never know, but realising that I might have plenty of spare time in the day, I also packed beads, cotton and needles so that I could carry on making my own costumes to fill my time. I also packed an odd book or two, not forgetting my small radio, with plenty of spare batteries, which turned out to be my saviour.

This time I arranged a direct flight to Cyprus, which meant I had to stay on the plane while it waited for an hour at Ismair Airport before it was able to fly off to Northern Cyprus. It seemed an easier option than the journey I had undergone with Helen a couple of months earlier, and the hour's wait at the airport was worth it. When the plane eventually set off on its last lap to Cyprus, I suddenly felt a sense of trepidation for the first time since I had made plans to make the journey and began to wonder if I had made the right decision.

I had been spoilt on my previous holiday, having been so well looked after by the brothers, but I realised this would be different as I did not know anybody there. Having only met Ibrahim the once, for a short spell, I was wondering what was ahead of me. There was no British Embassy out there to help if I might find myself in trouble as the UN kept the two countries, Northern Cyprus (occupied by the Turks) and the Republic of Cyprus (occupied by the Greeks), separated by the Green Line, preventing the ability to travel across the border – a big restriction and one that had to be adhered to.

I arrived safely at Lanarka Airport in Cyprus and was relieved to see Ibrahim waiting for me amongst the throng of people gathered, waving as he recognised me. He immediately put my belongings in the boot of his car and drove me to his home, without saying much on the way. He briefly introduced me to his family, but I felt a certain reticence from his wife and other members of his family, who I believe did not fully understand why I was there. I put it aside as Ibrahim showed me to my room at the back of the house, where I was to stay for the night, and asked me if I wanted something to eat. I explained that I had had something on the plane earlier, but he brought me a sandwich on a tray with a glass of fresh milk, which I was grateful for, and I settled down for the night.

I slept quite well and the next morning Ibrahim rushed me out of the house before I could say goodbye to members of his family, placing my belongings in the boot of his car telling me he would take me for a drive and show me around the island. He drove me to a park where we sat on a bench to enjoy the panoramic views and suddenly felt unprotected. He got hold of my hand, which I retrieved quickly from him, realising that I was in a vulnerable position. I told myself to remain as calm as possible. Then I explained to him that I had come all the way from the UK to dance at his taverna, which was agreed over the phone before I made the journey, and was the only reason I was there. I sensed he was not happy with that arrangement and acted as though he wanted me to satisfy his sensual side and tried to hold my hand. I let go, realising I had to get myself out of a tricky situation and, with no one around to help, I pretended I had a boyfriend who I was to marry on my return to the UK. It was not a complete untruth as I did have a boyfriend in the UK Colin, and even though I was not going to marry him, his name came in handy now and again! I could see that my disinterest in him was making him feel uncomfortable and we remained sitting on the bench without talking to one another. After a while, much to my relief, he suddenly got up, deciding we should get back in the car as he said he had got a friend to go and see.

I was grateful that the moment had passed but was concerned about whether he truly needed me as a dancer, and I began to wonder what I would do for six weeks out in Cyprus for all that time. We drove around for ages without talking and I began to think that he was wondering what to do with me. After a while he stopped and said, "You can stay here." He got my suitcases out from the back of his car and led me down a short garden to a place in complete rack and ruin. When he opened the door the smell of dust was acute, and an old unkempt bed was stuck in the middle of the room, surrounded by filthy old furniture that had been left abandoned. He gave me the keys and said, "I will see you tomorrow."

I could not sleep as the mattress – which I felt had been there since the beginning of time – was sticky and I knew there were insects and small animals in the room. In fact, I saw a lizard or a chameleon that looked at me with a beady eye and I could not believe what I was looking at. I just looked back in horror. When I turned my head for a split second, it had gone! After that I knew there were other beings in the room and gasped every time I heard a noise. There seemed to be sounds on the roof like birds and insects filtering through the structures and, being early August, it was hot and humid, with no air conditioning. There was an outside loo – just a hole in the ground loaded with cockroaches – and I thought I was having a bad dream.

The next morning, I was so glad to see the sunrise feeling I had survived the worst night of my life and patiently waited for Ibrahim to collect me. I waited and waited until it was midday, with still no sign, and feared that he had left me there with the intention of never seeing me again. Everyone in the UK had warned me about making the trip and was beginning to believe that I should have taken heed and listened to their concerns. But I was where I was, and had to think of what to do and realised I had no alternative but to venture from the dwelling and explore my surroundings.

I heard a lot of men at the end of the garden, who had accumulated outside a building next door. I did not know why they were there, but sensed they were aware of my presence in the premises and I just knew that I had to get out.

I did not want to go too far from the dwelling in case Ibrahim arrived and found I was not there, which would have been disastrous as there was no way of letting him know where I was. I closed the door behind me, clinging to the keys and began to walk past the queue of men eyeing me in a strange way. I put on a false air of confidence, hoping they would lay off the scent of my predicament, by walking with a purpose and avoiding their glances. The road seemed derelict and I passed many houses and bungalows, hoping somebody that I could speak to would open their door, but no one was about. It all seemed so quiet. I had walked a fair distance with not a car or a soul in sight and I grew very anxious, so much so that in the end I decided to knock on one of the doors to ask for help. I waited in the hope that someone would answer and eventually I heard footsteps and a lady opened the door to her bungalow, looking completely bemused at my presence. I explained that I needed the telephone, showing her Ibrahim's phone number and explaining that he had a taverna in Famagusta, but she had not heard of him and did not seem to understand what I was trying to say. I begged to use the phone as it was the only way I could contact him, insisting I would pay her for the call. She began to see the urgency in my request and kindly let me in. I was so grateful as she showed me where the phone was on the table in the hallway and waited around as I made the important call. The phone rang at the other end and I prayed Ibrahim would answer. I heard the phone lift, and it was his voice.

"Ibrahim, where are you? I've been waiting for you to collect me."

"Where are you?" he said.

I told him I had made the call from a lady's phone, whose name I did not know in one of the bungalows nearby, and that I had experienced a terrible night and needed his help to get away from the area and find somewhere better to stay. He could hear that I was under stress, understanding that I had gone to great lengths to get in touch with him, and he replied, saying that he would be on his way to collect me, and then put the phone down.

When I finished the call, I thanked the lady for all her help. She did not want anything for it but smiled and watched me leave as I made my way back to the shed, feeling conspicuous as I once again passed the group of young men, who were wondering what I was doing and why I was there.

Another hour or so went by as I sat outside in the hot blazing sun with all my belongings, when I heard a car stop at the front of the shed. It was Ibrahim; he had finally arrived. I was so relieved when I saw him, although he was not looking happy about the whole affair, as though he was still sulking from the day before, and he gave me the impression that I was a problem for him. He threw my suitcases in the boot of his car and drove me around as though he had nowhere to go, stopping and starting at different points and talking to friends on the way, who kept looking at me in the passenger's seat, grinning and wondering who I was.

He finally arrived at the large five-star Salamis Bay Hotel on the seafront and for a moment or two I began to believe that my fears were unfounded. He dumped my suitcases down on the beach with my other belongings, telling me he was leaving me there for the rest of the day but that he would be back later to collect me, and he drove off without any further explanation.

I clung to the hope that he would keep to his word, although I had no idea what time of day that would be or whether he would return at all, but I felt I was more in the land of the living, being on a sandy beach with people around me and hotel facilities nearby. I lay back on the sunbed, marvelling at the beautiful surroundings, listening to the tiny ripple of the waves slowly lap against the soft white silky sand when, before I knew where I was, I had dropped off into a deep sleep. Hours later, I woke up with a start to find I was the only person left on the beach. It did not take long to realise that Ibrahim had not returned as promised and I began to feel very confused about my circumstances.

I gathered myself together, trudging through the sand with my two suitcases and I managed to get them into the hotel foyer, where I found a seat and waited in the hope that Ibrahim would return to collect me. When it started to get dark, I used the phone at the hotel to try to contact him, but someone else answered in broken English, saying Ibrahim was not around but that he would pass my message on. As it got quite late into the evening, I was getting very concerned when the concierge at reception asked me if I was alright. I explained I was waiting for Ibrahim, who had asked me over from the UK to dance at his taverna and had left me at the hotel, without letting me know what time he was to collect me. The concierge felt that I had been treated unjustly and kindly got me a pot of tea, which was so welcome. As the evening wore on and I watched the clock tick by, my heart began to sink, recognising that he must have abandoned me and was not going to keep up with his part of the bargain. I had impulsively run away from a situation in the UK, taking the impetuous gamble of believing I could dance in another country on my own, not knowing a soul, without an agent, a proper booking or a contract and I was beginning to realise I had made a bad mistake.

By 11pm I had given up thinking Ibrahim would turn up, when the concierge approached me, saying he believed he might know Ibrahim and the taverna where he worked and asked me if I minded that he phone him to find out what was going on.

I was grateful for the offer and was surprised to hear that he got through to Ibrahim straight away talking in Turkish, and appeared to have a long banter with him before he waved me over to have a word with him. I let him know that I was worried about where I would stay that night not having booked anything, relying on his offer that he would look after me with board and lodging whilst I was over there, and that I did not have the funds to pay for a five-star hotel. His attitude had subsided somewhat; he sounded less aggrieved and said he would drive over straight away to collect me. I did not know if he genuinely felt responsible for my upkeep or whether he was worried about his name being branded about as he had a business to keep up, but whatever it was, I felt that this time he would keep to his word.

Not long after the call, he arrived with a look of thunder on his face. He threw my belongings into the boot of his car without a word and drove me into Famagusta, where he finally stopped at a little hotel down an alleyway. It was nearly midnight as he chatted to the hotel staff regarding a room and I waited in the car while they came to a decision about my staying there.

Eventually, my bags were taken upstairs by one of the hotel staff and I was shown to my room. It was heaven. At last, a twin bedroom, shower and WC, and a little table to write on. Absolute luxury.

The next morning the sun shone through the blinds and I opened the window, where I could see balconies littered with washing and the little street below with people popping into the shops and nattering with one another. I sniffed the Cyprus air, which was an absolute treat before the intense heat of the day.

After a little breakfast and a welcome coffee, I decided to

explore the area and find out where I was located. It was the centre of Famagusta, a bustling town with lots of little shops and cafés, where I stopped to have a cold drink every now and again as I was finding it difficult to accustom myself to the heat, especially by the middle of the day.

I bought myself some fruit and bread as I did not want to rely heavily on the hotel facilities and wandered around the town for most of the day, getting my bearings and arriving back at the hotel around 4pm, where, to my surprise, I found Ibrahim waiting for me in reception.

"You are alright?" he said.

"Yes, I'm fine. Thank you for putting me up here."

He gave me a half smile. It meant all was well between us. "I will take you to the taverna and show you about," he said.

It was a massive place and very different to how I remembered it when visiting it whilst with the brothers on holiday. The dance stage was like an airport. I imagined I would look like a pinprick in an ocean! There were rows upon rows of empty tables that could cater for hundreds of people.

"You will be OK working here," he said.

I remarked on the size of the stage and he laughed.

"Come, what would you like to eat – sheep's head?"

I looked at him, astonished, saying, "No… please."

He laughed and said it was a Cypriot delicacy, but instead he would get his chef to cook me kleftiko, a national dish. It was delicious. I was so hungry and washed it all down with a glass of "cankaya" dry white wine from Cyprus.

"You dance here, starting tomorrow night, yes?" That is what I had made the journey for and I was more than happy to accept. I asked if the band would know a piece of music that we both knew I could dance to rather than having to ad lib with music that I was not familiar with; being a large stage, a show performance at the beginning was necessary before engaging myself with the customers and I would need to return to the stage afterwards to end the show. He replied saying that he would introduce me to the members of the band beforehand so that there would be plenty of time to discuss those things before the show and said he would collect me the following evening at 8pm.

The next day in the morning, I asked reception if they could organise a taxi to drive me to the beach as it was difficult to get anywhere without public transport, which was limited. It pleased them that I chose to use the local taxi service from their hotel as it was part of their family concern, and I felt I was doing them a service by honouring them in that way.

I was able to get a lot of useful information from the taxi drivers, who gave me the names of many of the beaches I could visit around the area on the Turkish side of the island, and they never let me down when collecting me at an arranged time at the end of the day. I would have been in difficulties if they had as, being beach areas, telephones were not always easily accessible and relied on their service to get me around. I always tipped them well and they never let me down.

That night I wore one of my favourite cocktail dresses and waited at the bar in the hotel for Ibraham to collect me. Instead a stranger walked in, saying he was a friend of Ibrahim's and that he would take me to the taverna. He said his name was Yusuf and that he was a member of the band, playing the oud, and that we could discuss my entrance music, how long I might need to dance and the way I wanted to finish the show on our way there.

When we arrived at the taverna it was packed, the tables filled with customers, and I could hear Turkish music, laughter and people generally having fun. It looked so different from how I had seen it earlier in the day, barren and empty.

Ibrahim came up to me and said, "OK, change," and showed me a little room adjacent to the kitchen. It was just a larder with a curtain to hide behind and at first I felt uncomfortable in case someone might come in at a difficult moment! There was no air in there and being very hot, I felt the heat in the dressing room almost unbearable. I could hear the kitchen staff, a lot of them banging plates and singing as they washed up, but very happy with life and one another. I felt their attitude was catching so I joined in with their banter, speaking in English and hearing their laughter, whether they understood me or not.

Ibrahim gave me a nice length of time to change, which helped me to be mentally ready when it was my turn. A young lad came to collect me, leading me to where I was to wait in the wings as my announcement was being called, and then I heard my music start. There was a fair walk from the wings to the stage so I decided to make my way before my cue so that I would get on the stage in time, on the right beat. I always made it just on time! The stage was expansive. I had such an arena to move around and felt one had to be an athlete to make use of the space. The dance is really made up of body movements on the spot, with short steps now and again, but I tried to use the area by striding with large hip movements around the stage whilst swirling my veil the best I could. When it was the right time, I dropped the veil and left it behind on the stage so that I could join the customers, who were waiting for me to climb up on their tables which I sometimes wondered if they could hold my weight! Everyone was so obliging, smiling, friendly and laughing as I coped with all the scenarios, stepping on their plates of different mezes – which could not be avoided – but making my way by stepping from one table to the next unperturbed by any difficulties that could occur along the way.

I was absolutely littered with notes. They were of small denomination but it looked good and I was happy with whatever amount I could collect as it was already agreed in our unwritten contract that I could keep all the tips to myself.

After my show a lot of people came up to me, showing their

appreciation that I was visiting their country, and their gratitude meant a lot to me knowing I was accepted by them with their approval of my portrayal of their culture and dance.

Ibrahim appeared pleased with my performance and as I was sitting with the customers after the show, eating, drinking, dancing and generally enjoying their company, he made a point of coming over to tell me in front of everybody that I would get a lift back to the hotel and was to be collected the same time the next day.

★

Dancing in shows and staying up all night, sitting at the tables and joining in with the customers afterwards, made it all the more worthwhile to relax during the day on the beach, where I spent most of my time. Taxi fares cost me whilst travelling around which was my only expense as I did not have any hotel bills to pay and was saving a lot of money by eating and drinking at the taverna every night.

I had been at the hotel for just over a fortnight when, one early morning after my return from the taverna, I heard a knock on my door. It worried me and deliberately did not answer. I had kept myself to myself at the hotel, not getting to know the staff too well, which I felt was wise being a lady on my own there, so I was quite concerned that someone should be knocking at my door at that time in the morning. I could hear their footsteps in the hallway outside, walking about and waiting for me to open the door, but as time passed, whoever it was gave up and went away.

In the morning, downstairs in the vestibule, I was surprised to see Ibrahim waiting for me. "Get your belongings," he said bluntly. I did not ask any questions, I just did what I was told and collected my things. He speedily drove me to the Salamis Bay

Hotel area, where a friend of his owned a set of chalet houses next door to the hotel on the beach, where a unit had become available.

Whatever happened at the hotel resulting in my speedy removal worked out to be a blessing in disguise, for the change of accommodation was so much more suitable. I was right on top of a lovely sandy beach, which automatically saved a lot of money on taxi fares by not having to travel there and back. It was a smashing little chalet with everything I needed: twin beds, a shower, a little kitchen area with a stove and a little refrigerator, a table and two chairs. I could not have asked for more. It was perfect.

Before Ibrahim left, he explained that someone would collect me in the morning as there was a show he wanted me to do the following day.

★

As promised, Ibrahim collected me later the next day, but I was very surprised to see two UN officers seated in the front of a Bentley with a flag on the bonnet. I was told we were going into the ghost town area of Famagusta, where hundreds of Greeks fled without warning from their homes after the invasion by the Turks in 1974, with a lot of them having escaped to the southern side of the island.

I had met a lot of Cypriot customers from both the Turkish and Greek sides of the island in the clubs in London, who had shared their stories of what had happened to relatives of theirs in the wealthy beach resort of Varosha, but I was not fully prepared for the eerie experience that I was to envisage.

Ibrahim was sitting in the back of the car, smiling at me gingerly as I joined him. "Don't take any photographs, otherwise we could be arrested," he said. I laughed a little, not completely understanding the importance of his remark, but he nodded, saying, "Serious." I knew then the formality of the occasion and realised I would have to rely on my memory.

We arrived at the checkpoint where the general public were forbidden to enter, and the guards glanced at us in the back of the car before waving us on.

In 1925, the British took the land over and sold it to wealthy Greek entrepreneurs, who created a popular luxury holiday resort by the name of Varosha, where celebrities – including Elizabeth Taylor and Richard Burton – often frequented on their holidays.

In 1974, as revenge for the brutal uprisings by the Greeks in the 1960s – which caused devastation and catastrophe among the Turkish communities on the northern side of the island – the Turkish army parachuted down to retrieve their land in Famagusta, causing the Greeks, who were living there at the time, to escape from their homes, leaving all their belongings behind, fleeing in the clothes they wore, believing they would return one day. Not one bullet was fired throughout the operation and no one was killed or injured, but the area became a ghost town from that day onwards, and over the years it became entwined in the difficult dilemma of who could claim the area. It was originally charitable land owned by the Ottoman Empire, and the quandary of compensation for who owns the land is still a riddle for the lawyers as the Title of the land belongs to the Ottoman Turkish Charitable Foundation, which makes it look like Turkey holds the cards for reaching an amicable settlement. In the meantime, the land remains closed to the public until a workable settlement can be achieved.

As we started out on our journey, I was trying to untie the time warp of many years earlier, when the invasion took place. We drove through miles of open waste land, dead to the world, and through desolate residential areas of unoccupied property, overgrown gardens and unkempt pasture, unloved and forgotten. Once well-established villas disintegrated and tumbled apart, allowing fully grown trees to emerge through the roofs of buildings. We saw old furniture relics fading, broken and crumbling into dust. A Barclays bank stood empty, abandoned just like the churches left to rot and the hotels in the town centres, once fully occupied and buzzing with life, now derelict, without a sound; crates outside still piled high with empty bottles, the contents of which had evaporated in the intense heat. Cups and saucers were strewn on crooked tables outside coffee houses, some broken, some just left as they lay.

The silence was heavy; not a sound cracked the air. There were no animals or birds, or the rustling of a rat scrambling in the undergrowth, just an empty eeriness of life in deep decay.

My pride of being driven in a Bentley with a flag on the front dissipated very speedily as I realised there was no one around to see us.

Suddenly we arrived at a beautiful location – a luxury hotel, unspoilt, in all its glory, shining like marble, majestic and proud in the middle of nowhere.

We were escorted into a dining area where tables had been laid for a banquet and were introduced to three important officers: the Admiral of the Fleet, beautifully dressed from head to toe in a white uniform, a lieutenant colonel and a squadron leader. We all shook hands very politely but the atmosphere felt formal and I noticed that Ibrahim appeared very uncomfortable.

In the corner of the dining room was a small band of three who lacked lustre in their appearance and the Admiral of the Fleet asked me if there was a piece of music I would like to dance to. I chose 'Azziza' because even though it's well known in the Arabic countries, it is familiar with most Middle Eastern musicians. To my amazement, at that moment, the regimental band started to play the music I had asked for. I am sorry to say that it was possibly the tinniest and most characterless interpretation I had ever heard of that beautiful piece of music, but not wanting to show my displeasure under the circumstances, I congratulated them for their performance. I had come across occurrences before where some bands were not adequately able to play Arabic music for a dancer, but my motto on those occasions was to forget the music and just dance!

The show went well considering it was a male officer-only audience – there were hundreds of them sitting at tables, all very orderly and above board – and I was asked to get on a few tables to dance, where they were generous with their tips and made sure that I was well looked after.

Ibrahim and I sat with some of the officers for the rest of the evening until it was time for us to leave, when we were glad to return to the waiting Bentley and depart from that depressing area. The night had already set in, with the atmosphere becoming noticeably dense. There was nothing about and the silence was deafening. The only lighting came from the headlights of the car as we drove back through the haunted wasteland, sensing a threatening gloom around us, almost frightening, not having a sense of where we were or where we were going. Then gradually, in the far distance, we saw tiny lights shining from the town of Famagusta – a welcome sight – as we eventually approached the checkpoint to pass through security to leave the area. I came away wishing that I had a magic wand to wave over that part of Cyprus in the hope that an amicable settlement could one day be made to solve the dilemma, and that everyone could enjoy that part of the world again.

★

I slept well on my second night in the chalet and the next

morning I sauntered straight onto the beach, thinking how marvellous it was not having to rely on taxis to get me around, and dug my toes in the sand as I ventured along the shoreline to see what I could find. There were plenty of young men walking back and forth along the beach, giving me the odd glance, but never returned the acknowledgement as I did not want to get attached to anyone. In any case, I was recovering from a broken relationship and trying to find myself, and knew it was something only I could do on my own. I must have walked a couple of miles along the beach when I found a taverna just off from the sea, up some steps on a hill. I fancied a Coke as it was very hot, being the middle of the day, and sat down at one of the empty tables to enjoy the view. Looking around, I noticed that there was an area especially created for a small band and wondering if they might need a dancer in the evenings, I took the initiative to ask one of the waiters if I could meet the owner. I did not have to wait long before an elderly gentleman with a large white moustache came walking towards me, smiling and introducing himself, saying he was Mr Bedis the same name as the taverna, that he had worked at Wheelers in London for many years and his skills as a chef were well known in the area.

I explained I had come from England and was performing at Ibrahim's taverna most nights, but that I wondered if he needed a dancer to fit in with my other bookings. He laughed at first but to my surprise said yes as he had a live band there every so often and as my lodgings were not far away, it was agreed that I would dance there on a flexible basis on the nights he was busy.

He was a very generous, jovial sort of chap, leaving his door open for me to pop round and visit whenever I was in the area, which was so convenient as he was just along the beach to where I was staying in the chalet near the hotel. He had many influential friends in the Cypriot community from all over the island who frequently visited his taverna to share a meze and a glass of wine with him, and I was always welcome to join them, enjoying many an afternoon meeting different people from all walks of life in the Cypriot community until the sun slowly set in the evening. Mr Bedis and I got to know each other quite well during my stay there and he offered to drive me around the island during the day to show me some of the sights and introduce me to some of his friends who were living in Kyrenia and Nicosia.

He also took me to a casino on the coastline of Famagusta, Palma Hotel, where one of his friends was working and treated me to some chips to play with. I had not told him that I knew how to play roulette reasonably well due to an uncle who had bought me a roulette ensemble from France when I was a girl and, against my parents' wishes, I had spent time practising spins and methods, finding a system where I believed I could win. But that was in home surroundings. The game is a different beast when playing it for real at the casino; I was told by an experienced croupier once, whether true or not, that most tables have magnets planted under them, apart from one table where no one plays as it is usually a fair distance away from the other established tables, generally surrounded by staff, as though guarded from public use. As no one knew my skill, if one can call gambling a skill, I decided to use a simple method by placing my chips on either black or red, a 50/50 option, rather than using a 'system', and as I had spotted that the ball had already landed on red for the last five occasions, I gambled by putting all my chips on black. I watched the expertise of the croupier as he tossed the tiny ball in the opposite direction of the turn of the wheel, as it flew around the top of the face until it lowered itself, bubbling and jumping over the numbered slots before it sat politely in its chosen pocket where it waited for the wheel to stop. "No.3 – black!" was called out and I knew I had been lucky. There was a lot of laughing around the table, with people wondering what I would do next, and as the original bet was not mine in the first place I had the courage to gamble on the same bet again, but keeping my winnings safe. "No.29 – black." The table was running well for me. By now, I was getting serious looks from around the table, but I decided to leave the original chips on black again as a final throw and waited, hoping my luck would not change. "No.11 – black." It was a wonderful feeling – hurray, I had won for the third time – and that was as lucky as I felt I dare be. The table can be cruel with one who becomes too confident and blasé, that's how punters get caught and how casinos capture their victims, so I decided to cash in whilst ahead. It meant I was able to return my original bet to Mr Bedis, who beamed at the good fortune his chips had achieved, and I could tell he was wondering whether he ought to have a 'go' with the same chips I had used before cashing in.

The days were lazy with a small routine: lying on the beach relaxing, listening to the BBC Home Service on my little radio whilst patiently threading beads for my new costumes, gently strolling along the beach at midday to meet with Mr Bedis who would introduce me to another guest that had joined him for a light lunch during the day, and preparing myself for shows later in the evening, where I would usually stay until the early hours of the morning.

★

Over the years I had experienced a recurring dream where I would walk through a car park near some little shops with families walking around happily exploring the area, with a café or restaurant on a hillside up from a sandy beach, where I would find myself walking by a jetty. At the beginning of the dream I felt at peace as I walked along the beach in an idyllic location but every time I approached the jetty, I would sense a great sadness and depression that I could never understand, especially when I was in such wonderful surroundings.

When I sensed the dream approaching, I tried with great difficulty to drag my mind away from it, as I became aware of the deception of enjoying a paradise only to feel a sense of loss at the end of it, but found I was constantly drawn back into it, whichever way I tried to avoid it, and reluctantly went along with the flow of it, knowing full well I would inevitably end up in the same place by the jetty and overwhelmed by the same feelings of loss and sadness.

I had tucked the dream away in my consciousness, as I was only reminded of it when it happened in a dream, but one day, whilst admiring the view at the Bedis Taverna, idly watching a young man dive from the end of the jetty successfully time and time again, I realised on the last occasion when he dived that he had not emerged from the sea for a fair length of time. I became agitated on not seeing the young man rise from the water when suddenly there was a flurry of activity from the bathers on the beach, yelling and shouting. Two waiters from the taverna suddenly tore down the hillside, tearing their shirts off to dive into the sea, swimming their hearts out to the spot where the man had jumped. Every second felt like an hour.

They found him and carried him out, each holding an arm, with his head still dragging in the water. It was plain to see he was not breathing.

There were many attempts to revive him but there was no movement and eventually the police arrived, putting a white sheet over the body and cleared the area. Before long a silent crowd of bathers accumulated around Mr Bedis' taverna in a terrible state of shock.

It was such a macabre sight to see a lonely corpse, having lost his life within seconds, lying on an idyllic spot with the sun beating down, the rhythmic tones of the tiny waves of the sea gently touching the white powdered sand as they had done moments before he jumped.

What made it more nonsensical was the fact that the medic van was too short for the length of his body and as the van took the corpse away, the young man's legs were in full view, hanging out at the back. Such an undignified end.

Apparently, he was a local Turkish Cypriot who had hit his head on a rock after his dive, making him unconscious. It was printed in the local Cypriot newspapers the next day that he had left a Finnish wife and two children. I never had that dream again.

★

Ibrahim organised for me to dance at a Turkish Army barracks, taking his band from the taverna. He was to perform as the lead Turkish singer.

We all managed to squeeze into the same car and trekked off into an unfamiliar part of Cyprus with no landmarks for me to acquaint myself with until we arrived at the barracks in the dead of the night, where we were greeted by a bevy of army officers who had been patiently waiting for our arrival. We were immediately ushered up some rickety wooden stairs to a makeshift dining room, where there were some tables informally laid out for a party.

The band and Ibrahim took their place on the stage, where they tried to rev up an atmosphere as the place started to slowly fill with army clientele, guests and friends. The officers had an air of authority that one would expect, but there were many young lads waiting on us looking nervous, somewhat gaunt with shaved heads, looking blankly into the distance, in contrast to the portly officers who were immaculate in dress and flourishing in confidence.

The time came for me to do my show and I was led down the wooden stairs by an army corporal to a tiny room to change. The officer stood guard outside the door, when I realised I needed to go to the loo before my show, which caused a difficulty as they had not considered I might need one.

I was already in my costume, covered by a flimsy veil, as the officer led me to another set of wooden stairs descending downwards to the ground floor, with soldiers standing to immediate attention on different landings of the staircase, clicking their heels and saluting as we passed. I politely thanked them but felt very out of place. After passing many soldiers, the officer yelled out to a closed door and a nervous cadet came out doing up his trousers. The aroma of the toilet was horrendous. It was in a deplorable state and my breath was taken away for a moment, but there was nothing I could do. I needed the loo. When I came out, the officer walked back with me up the stairs to the dressing room, shouting orders all the way to obedient young men saluting dutifully as I passed, which they had been trained to do.

Finally, I was led up the next set of stairs recognising my music beginning its theme, so I clinked my finger cymbals and made my way onto the stage, much to the delight of the army elite. They were less formal than the UN officers in Famagusta for whom I had danced previously, openly showing they were enjoying themselves. I was a little nervous about whether the tables might be secure enough to hold my weight, but unperturbed, the officers helped me up onto the chairs to get on the tables without mishap and the army clientele made sure that I made plenty of tips to make up for my journey.

After the show there was a raffle and I won a blue cigarette ashtray, which I collected from the stage and still have to this day. Strangely, only having been present at two big raffles in my life, I won on both occasions with the same number, No.11, which had also shown to be a lucky number on the roulette wheel at the casino with Mr Bedis. Perhaps I should have gambled with that number more often!

★

I was nearing the end of my visit to Cyprus and whilst on the beach reflecting on my stay and busy working on my beads, a man called Mehmet approached me, asking if I was Shariffa, the belly dancer he had heard about. I explained that it might be because I was not aware of another dancer with that name in the area and asked him what he wanted. He politely asked if he could sit next to me as he had a proposition he wanted to put before me.

He was arranging a circumcision party for his son in the village called Topcukoy high up in the mountains near Nicosia where he lived and wondered if I would agree to do a show for him. I knew it to be a fair distance away from Famagusta, where I was staying, and explained that I was concerned about organising taxis to get there, considering I had other bookings in different places that night, and as it was my last evening in Cyprus before catching the 6am flight to Turkey to get back to the UK, I did not think I could dare take the risk.

He insisted, saying it was a special occasion for his son and that the show would be videoed with the whole village attending, including a small band that had been organised for the event. Then he told me he would pay me well to dance and would organise a taxi from Salamis Bay Hotel to take me to the village, as he knew someone at the taxi rank who would look after me, and take me back to the airport after the show.

It was a complete gamble. I had timed the other shows to fit in with my flight and this was in a place I had never heard of which meant trusting a stranger again, but instinct told me he was a good man, and I sensed he truly wanted this to be a special occasion for his son that would be remembered for the rest of his life. He waited but then started to plead with me to make my decision, saying it would please him so much if I would do it. So, I agreed.

My last day had to be timed like a well-tuned clock, carefully organised and with no leeway for delays.

I packed my bags and suitcases, which were bursting at the seams, and Ibrahim's assistant collected me to dance at his taverna for my last show.

It was an emotional parting; we had both come a long way. "I'll come to the UK," he said with a massive grin on his face. I grinned back and thanked him for the wonderful time I had experienced working for him and got in the waiting car, where I waved goodbye to him through the back window.

Then I arrived at the Bedis Taverna, which was packed with guests enjoying themselves. I danced around the tables, finishing with a bow, and Mr Bedis smiled at me so sweetly after the show and said I must return to do the whole thing again one day. He arranged for one of his waiters to take me to my next venue and as we drove down the dusty roads, I saw Mr Bedis fade further and further away into the distance until I could not see him anymore.

Arriving at the Hotel Rebecca, music was playing loudly in the outside forecourt and danced to a wonderful audience around a swimming pool, making lots of tips. Fortunately, I did not fall in the pool as I cannot swim! After the show a waiter kindly gave me a lift to Salamis Bay Hotel, where I was to pick up a taxi to get me to Topcukoy village in the mountains.

I had not been in touch with Mehmet after we met on the beach as he had not left me a telephone number to contact him, but just the name of the village on a piece of paper and the date and time he wanted me to arrive. He told me that he worked at the Salamis Bay Hotel and that he would have a taxi waiting for me but there were so many taxis there, I could not work out which driver he had organised for me, and in the end I asked an unknown driver if he knew of the village. He said he did, but that it was quite a long drive. I managed to convince the driver that I needed to get to the village for a circumcision party that had been arranged for Mehmet's son, and that the hosts were waiting for me. He realised I was sincere and put my suitcases in the boot of the car with the understanding that I was catching a flight immediately after the show, early in the morning.

The journey seemed never ending. There was nothing to see. It was dark, with no lighting along the bumpy, dusty roads apart from a full moon that night, emphasising black mountains that were eerily shrouded in darkness far in the distance. I had no idea where I was, where I was going or what the village would be like when I got there, but the driver and I chatted to fill the time. He was friendly and affable enough but being in such a desolate place, with not a soul around, there were moments when I felt a little vulnerable.

Then, out of the blue, I saw some lights and activity in the distance, which was a comfort, and at long last we arrived at the centre of the village where Mehmet came to greet me. I was so pleased to see him.

He sat me down next to an old lady wearing a long shawl and even though she could not speak a word of English, she befriended me with her smiles and beady playful eyes. I do not think she had any idea why I was at the venue, but she probably thought I was a guest or a tourist of some sort for the occasion.

Then I recognised Erdinch behind the video camera. I had seen him before at one of the shows, but it was an opportunity to ask for a copy of the video if he would be kind enough to send me one, and I gave him my address and some money for the postage.

The band was jolly enough – a lot more fun than other bands I had come across – and the whole of the village was seated outside in a semi-circle, meticulously arranged for the purpose. The area was remote with treacherous, dusty, uneven ground, as though space on the mountain range had been allotted for the occasion with no modern facilities.

The lighting in the area was flimsy and dim and Mehmet asked me to get ready. I climbed some wooden stairs to a small hut where there was a tiny room I could change in. Then I could hear my name being announced. "We have a special guest – Shariffa." I began to rattle my finger cymbals in tune with the band and gently felt my way down the wooden stairs to the bumpy ground below. I danced barefoot, as I always did, taking care where I stepped on the treacherous ground as it was full of potholes and I had to be extremely careful, which thwarted the freedom I needed when dancing. Then I approached a solemn, beautiful little boy, who was lying in a gigantic king-size bed all to himself, surrounded by toys that had been given to him by the guests as presents, and I released my veil by the side of him, which he touched with his tiny little hands.

The stage area was so uneven, it was impossible to dance without fear of slipping or breaking my ankle, and I kept my eye on my footing as best I could as I had already survived two months out in Cyprus without mishap or injury and, considering it was my last show, I was determined not to fall foul of the precarious situation just before my flight back to the UK.

I managed to make a show of it although the drummer and I found it difficult to synchronise at the end for the finale, not knowing each other's movements, which, without lots of practice between the drummer and the dancer, was not unusual, but there was one thing I wanted to do before leaving the stage and that was to say goodbye to the little old lady I had sat next to earlier. I ran over to her, giving her a kiss on both cheeks, which, much to my surprise, caused a rumpus in the audience with the band jollying the music again and everyone ecstatically hooping and whistling around me. I begged her to get up and walk towards the little boy in his large bed, which she did not want to do at first, but the audience was behind me and helped me to convince her to get up. I waited and waited, then she finally rose from her seat and followed me to the little boy in the bed, where she sat down, and I danced around them for a while.

At that moment I was besieged and covered in notes. The audience would not stop planting more in my costume. It was an emotional moment. I hugged the old lady again and tried to finish with a finale to a band who did not know when to stop playing, grabbed my veil from the bed where the little boy lay and ran up the stairs to change.

Mehmet had organised a taxi for me to return to the airport, reassuring me it was all paid for, and the friendly driver drove me safely and soundly in the early hours of the morning to Lanarca Airport, just in time to catch my plane. It was a lovely way to finish off my trip to Cyprus and I was so glad to receive a video of the whole event a month after I arrived back in the UK.

*

My problems were not fully over because even though I was in time to catch my flight from Cyprus to Turkey, which went smoothly enough, I had a six-hour wait at Istanbul airport before I was to board my flight back to the UK.

I found that my suitcases were not on the turntable and as time passed by, I knew there was a problem. I started walking around the airport frantically looking for some guidance or help, but no one seemed to be able to advise me. There were many armed soldiers at the airport with two women soldiers at the bottom of a staircase who pulled their Kalashnikov rifles as I tried to climb the steps they were guarding. They let me go, but there was nothing up there other than corridors with a lot of closed doors. The surroundings appeared austere and I felt uneasy, as though I was being watched, but all I was worried about was trying to find my suitcases that seemed to have gone missing.

Disappointed with not finding anything upstairs, I went down the stairs, passing the women soldiers to check the turntable again, but I did not find anything and my heart sank believing I had lost all my costumes and belongings.

I began to walk aimlessly around the airport, hoping to get a clue where my cases might be, but I was none the wiser and decided to go up the stairs again, what for I had no idea, but as I attempted to do so the women soldiers got hold of their rifles and barred me from going any further. I tried to explain that I had lost my suitcases and needed help. They did not understand but surprisingly retrieved their rifles, letting me pass. I knew, though, that it would have to be the last time I tried. In my dilemma I decided to knock on one of the closed doors down the corridor and entered one of the offices to find four or five men sitting at desks, looking fully engrossed in what they were doing. No one looked up or seemed bothered about my entering the room except for one man. "What is it?" he said in English and I spurted out that I needed help. He took me out into the hallway, hearing the rest of my story and left me, saying, "OK."

I honestly did not know what to expect. He was my last hope because there was nothing else I could do. I sat down and watched the passengers walking about with their suitcases for a while with the worry that there was no news of mine, and tried to come to terms with the fact that I would have to board my flight without them. In fact, I had resigned myself to the inevitable, that my suitcases had gone, and was reflecting on the thought that at least it had happened after my stay rather than before I arrived in Cyprus, which would have been a worse catastrophe.

I do not know what made me do it, but I got up from where I was sitting to look over the railings at the airport and to my utter astonishment, a porter wheeling my suitcases on a trolley caught my eye. I was ecstatic; they had been found. It did not take long to be reunited with them and I was so grateful. A weight had been lifted from my shoulders and I wish to this day that I had been able to thank that lovely man in the office who helped me.

I got them weighed in for my flight and then my hand luggage had to be checked. Stern duty officers went through my things with a fine-tooth comb. I had stupidly left a pair of large scissors at the bottom of my handbag rather than put them in the suitcase. The airport attendant took them out without a word, put a sticker on them and tossed them aside. I looked at him and explained that they had sentimental value as they were my mother's and asked if he could let me have them back, never believing I had a chance of retrieving them. The attendant seemed to look right past me, as though I was not there. Not a muscle moved on his face as his arm edged towards the scissors, putting them back into my handbag without saying a word. I was astonished at what he had done and thanked him, but he remained as motionless as he was when he began. It was certainly my lucky day.

I boarded the plane and could not remember the trip. I just slept on and off for the whole journey, which was remarked on by the hostesses, until I arrived back in England without a mac or an umbrella, which I desperately needed because it was raining, and I was shivering with the cold!

★

Returning to the Chalayan felt disorientating in many ways, bringing back old memories that I had hoped would have disappeared after my trip to Cyprus, because I kept reflecting on how wonderful it would have been to have returned to the restaurant as it was in my earlier days. But on the other hand, the break had taught me to accept that the place was under new management, with a different approach and style, and as the previous owner had left the premises, I was to look upon it as a fresh start.

I wanted to keep busy, not dwell on the past, and also got another job in Victoria, London, where I danced in a Greek club every Friday and Saturday night, performing to a live band until the early hours of the morning. There was a vibrancy in the atmosphere at the club, with plenty of wealthy customers who gave generously and I danced to packed audiences, sometimes more than once in the night. There were no strict rules as to what time I was to dance as I could arrive or leave at any time of my choice and I was able to sit with the customers after my show if I wished to enjoy their company, eating, drinking and dancing with them, all in light-hearted fun, until I left at around five in the morning.

Whilst dancing at these venues, I was still able to work for the secretarial agency during the week, and Ingrid sent me to an old, established firm of solicitors called Radcliffes, near the Houses of Parliament. I was only there a couple of days but to my surprise I saw Ms Jay Benning, the lady solicitor and senior partner I was working for as a temp at the beginning of my dancing career in Portland Place. She had become a consultant and was sitting in the reception area, ready to be picked up by her driver. I recognised her haughty air but noticed she had aged considerably; she was looking frail and clutching a stick whilst resting in a Chesterfield leather chair. She was alone but I decided to take the courage to approach her knowing I would regret it if I did not make the effort, thinking I might never see her again. She did not seem to mind and smiled as I spoke to her.

"You won't remember me," I said, "but I was a temp in your firm of solicitors a long while back, about ten years ago, working for your husband, the litigation partner at the time." She looked at me with curious eyes, to see if she could recollect me. I decided to tell her the details of what had happened whilst I was working at her firm because I felt she was worldly enough to appreciate the story. I told her that at the time I was also training to be a belly dancer and that Ingrid had given me an opportunity of dancing at the Christmas buffet lunch for the temporary secretaries at the Cavendish Personnel Agency. By now she was listening intently, remembering Ingrid and the agency, whom she knew well at the time. I explained that I was very nervous about doing the show as it had only been my second appearance in public but as Ingrid had proposed an extended lunch hour for the purpose, I felt I had to agree to her offer. I could see she was enjoying the fact that I was taking the trouble to talk to her and she seemed fascinated about the subject. I carried on, "I did not know whether I should tell you, but as it was such a surprise to see you after all these years, I could not keep it to myself."

She looked at me, wondering what was coming next. "Please carry on," she said.

I told her that I had been expecting to dance in front of a crowd of other temporary secretaries but to my surprise, as I entered the arena to face the audience, guess who was there amongst the girls.

"I have no idea," she remarked.

"Your husband," I said. "Yes, your husband had taken time off to come to the Christmas buffet lunch and he was the only man in the group."

Her face suddenly cracked into a loud laugh as she could see the funny side of things. "No," she said.

"Well," I carried on, "I got him out to dance and I put my veil around his waist, and he joined in." She carried on laughing, thoroughly enjoying what she was hearing. "He took the stage," I told her, and then I asked her to thank him for having the courage to come that day, as he was star of the show and we all enjoyed his contribution.

Her eyes glistened. "I will. I will go home tonight and over dinner I will tell him that I have found out what he did behind my back," she said in amusement. "He never told me, you see." We both chuckled about it, all in jest, until her driver came to collect her to take her home.

★

Over the next three years, I kept up with my secretarial duties during the day whilst dancing at the Greek club in Victoria and the Chalayan at the weekends, besides dancing in many restaurants and other venues in London when the need arose, but I was beginning to feel that I had become as professional as I was ever going to be and that I had achieved as much as I wished to achieve, and began to question myself as to why I was doing the shows. That sense of joy that had inspired me in the beginning, that drive and energy that satisfied that unknown need to succeed, that part of myself that needed to be explored, just wasn't there any more. Sometimes I found it more of a job than a joy, relying on technique to see me through rather than being inspired by that sense of magic that once immersed my energy in the earlier days. I was beginning to ask myself what more I needed to prove!

Whilst I was between dancing posts but still working at the Chalayan on Saturday nights, Ingrid phoned me, hoping I would accept a secretarial position that another agency had passed to her, which she was eager to fill as it seemed a lot of girls had turned it down for some reason or another. As I thought it would be a good time to take a break from my heavy dancing schedule, being an unusual offer, I accepted the challenge.

It was to work for John Mowlem Construction Plc, one of the largest building companies in the UK at the time. They were looking for a replacement secretary as a matter of urgency.

The offices were opposite the Charles Dickens Museum in Doughty Street, just off from Gray's Inn Road. It was an open booking and I was to join two other secretaries in the main reception area. The offices were roomy with high ceilings, nicely decorated and well equipped, with function rooms overlooking gardens at the back of the building, where buffet lunches were often administered to draw in new business projects for clients and guests.

Jacky, the principal secretary, besides having admin duties, was specially trained to organise events for large groups of people and had a knowledge of preparing buffets – and other catering needs – for such gatherings, as well as a course in flower arranging as an extra craft thrown in.

The directors of the company were housed in rooms on the ground floor, with surveyors occupying the upper floors, and not forgetting the buyers residing in a department all to themselves on the top floor. It was a busy, bustling place, with the phone ringing all day long, as the office was the main hub and headquarters for all the staff on different sites in the company.

Once or twice a week, we three secretaries would have to share in the preparation of laying the tables in the function rooms for those occasions by using the facilities that were stocked in the kitchen downstairs, and on the day of the event, luxury catering companies would arrive with baskets full of food already prepared, which they carefully laid out on the tables. It was noticeable how the atmosphere would change quite suddenly from an office routine into one of a social nature as the guests gradually arrived, and it was our duty to lead them to where they needed to go and introduce them to one another.

As the events lingered into the early afternoon, we could clearly hear their voices heightening as they shared stories together, with frequent bursts of laughter pealing in chorus that echoed down the corridor. We were tied to our desks with the burden of ploughing through heavy loads of work that were expected to be completed by the end of the day, and hearing the frivolity of a party atmosphere not far from our office sometimes clashed with our concentration. We were also kept busy answering the telephones and took it in turns delivering important messages to those we could find amidst the visitors.

When the party was in full throttle and some of the food was taken downstairs for refrigeration, Jacky took the initiative to see what she could salvage from the leftovers, rushing back to the office with plates of sandwiches, tasty morsels, cakes and snacks for us to enjoy as we remained at our desks. It was a welcome treat that no-one denied us, as few noticed what we had on our desks by the end of the afternoon.

The whole experience was so different to working in a legal office, which I sometimes found could be challenging, especially when dealing with heavy personalities who had a way of imposing their presence, testing their humour and communicative chatter, but once it was understood that a sense of humour was imperative, everything fell into place.

*

As my new secretarial role appeared to be taking a lot of my time, I tried to keep my dancing to a minimum so that I could manage both careers, when quite suddenly, Ali told me one weekend that he was deciding to sell the Chalayan to someone who would not be carrying on with the same business. In many ways, I was expecting his decision as he had been complaining recently of how hard restaurant life was, openly admitting fatigue from all the late nights. He explained that he felt it was time to take an early retirement.

I had worked there for over ten years, mainly with Ata until Ali took over, and my heart had always been closely linked with the Chalayan through all the joys and sadnesses connected with it over the years; no other place emotionally affected me in the same way. It had been the nucleus of my strange journey into a world I never knew existed, yet, with the news that the Chalayan was now in the process of being sold, never to be again, I somehow felt it was time to say goodbye, and accepted that it was the end of an era.

★

I had been working at John Mowlem & Co. for six months when one of the directors, David Liming, was about to take on a project at the Guildhall to recreate the east wing into a new art gallery, a great responsibility. I was astonished when he asked me if I would like to be his PA. It meant becoming permanent and leaving the cosy offices in Doughty Street to work on-site, which was a big decision, but as I was not as committed to my dancing career as I had been, other than at the weekends, the proposal came at the right time and as it sounded an exhilarating challenge, and decided to accept.

I arrived at the Guildhall not knowing what to expect and was asked who I was by a chap wearing a hard hat at the entrance gateway. He had a walkie talkie that leant on his shoulder and spoke through the mouthpiece to David Liming, who I heard say, "Bring her up," on the other end of the phone. I was told to follow the structure of the manmade steps all the way up to the top of the scaffolding, where David was to meet me. I held onto the metal handrails, made up of steel tubes, noticing that I could see beneath me through the iron stairs onto the forecourt below. I progressed climbing upwards and eventually arrived at the first makeshift landing, where I heard David shouting from above that I had to get to the next level.

The steps shook slightly as I carried on upwards until I stopped to take a breather, when I looked over the side of the railings to observe the Guildhall courtyard, filled with builders and trucks that were delivering and unloading a concoction of supplies, including the famous Portland Stone in even slabs, which was especially brought in from Dorset.

As I approached the top of the staircase, I hardly recognised David. He was wrapped in a large yellow fluorescent jacket and was wearing big boots. A red hard hat covered his blonde hair as he stood there smiling at me. "We will have to get you equipped," he said out loud. "You will need two hard hats, a blue one for the NatWest Tower," (a project opposite the Bank of England, where he was also a director) "and a red one for the Guildhall."

Our footsteps echoed along the flimsy wooden planks that acted as a temporary landing before we arrived at the portacabin that I was to share with a group of men sitting at desks on their computers. Nigel Barker, a friendly document controller, immediately got up from his desk to shake my hand, smiling heartily as David introduced me as his PA secretary. I was shown to where I would be sitting and was impressed that a reception area, fully equipped with a desk and computer, was all set up for my arrival. Then I could not help but notice a pretty ensemble of plastic flowers of all different colours that had been neatly arranged in a glass vase as a focus point on my desk. "Oh, how lovely, aren't they pretty?" I remarked and I could see that my words were valued as Nigel insisted it was his wife's work whilst winking at David, who seemed surprised, saying it was his wife who had arranged the ensemble, but it did not matter who it was as I appreciated the gesture in any case.

We were based in a portacabin on top of another portacabin as space was limited in the forecourt at the Guildhall, which gave a sense of slight swaying, as though being on board ship, which effects lingered well after leaving the site at the end of the day and took a while to get used to. A photocopy machine monopolised the main area of the cabin as it played an important role in the everyday working process of the project, in that every piece of paper that passed through my fingers had to be copied ten or more times for distribution. A never-ending flow of paperwork was circulated around so everyone on site could share each other's knowledge of each stage in the process. Wooden pigeonhole boxes with the names of heads of departments in all fields were stacked high in rows especially for that purpose, and I was intrigued at the extent of furnishings and office equipment that could be stored in such a small enclosure, including space for meeting rooms and an office for David at the other end of the cabin.

There were approximately three hundred men on-site, and I was the only woman. A pair of boots had to be specially made for my shoe size being 4½, as the company only catered for men with much larger feet.

In the morning I took shorthand notes of instruction from David before I was able to start work on anything else. It was a hectic role, checking all the deliveries that arrived on site, churning out snagging lists, photocopying faxes, drawings and delivery receipts – the paperwork was immense – and answering the phones, which rang all day long, besides looking after guests who would visit the site. To my amusement, I learnt how to keep a conversation between the calls, lasting a second or two before the next call, which almost became second nature.

When visitors arrived, it was my duty to equip them with hard hats and boots, which we had stored in the portacabin, before they could be shown around the site by David. As I helped them try things on for size, which did not always fit, the process often caused a lot of laughter as some had to make do with what was on offer. On their return, they were escorted into a special meeting room at the back of the portacabin to discuss the next stages of the project, and I managed to make pots of tea from a small water urn on the level below, which I placed in a cardboard box with plastic cups, a carton of milk and sugar lumps in a tin. It was all very improvised and difficult to balance as I climbed back up the scaffold steps to return to the portacabin, where I kept a packet of biscuits in my desk for those occasions, and when I entered the meeting with my homemade tea set, seeing how grateful they all appeared made the effort so worthwhile.

On miserable days when the weather was bad, the rain would cascade down the main door of the cabin and men would invariably walk in and out as they pleased, balancing their walkie talkies on their shoulders, dripping with rain from head to foot, shuffling around on the floorboards in their large muddy boots. I was always impressed by the bravery of some of those men who were locked in boxes on the top of high cranes, sometimes taking refuge in the portacabin from the wind and rain for a short spell before they returned to the heights of that iron ladder in the sky.

Fire drills were frequent due to the concern of the authorities that so much unusual activity was happening in the precincts of the Guildhall, and we were constantly on the alert, ready to leave at a moment's notice if anything was untoward, wearing our hard hats and clambering down the scaffolding from one level to the next to join the men already gathered in the courtyard below, where different group leaders would shout out names from a list, making sure all were present before the OK was given to get back to work again.

Popular events at the Guildhall still took place whilst building works were in process, and in our lunch hour Nigel and I would sometimes take the opportunity of observing what was going on. On one occasion we were fortunate enough to witness Norman Wisdom being awarded the Freedom of the City, with newspaper reporters present, flying around taking pictures of him as he smiled for the cameras, obviously delighted with the accolade allotted to him. Most of the Mowlem staff adored the vintage car shows, which were splendid affairs, to name but a few special occasions whilst I was there.

When we reached a certain stage of the project at the NatWest Tower, David asked me to organise the topping out, which was a special occasion in the diary of a new construction project.

I went to Tesco down Cheapside, borrowing two hefty builders from the site to help carry back sandwiches, wraps, crisps, cakes and biscuits, and a variety of wines and beers for the guests who might want something stronger, not forgetting party plates and napkins. We laid it out in a somewhat amateur manner on plastic tables that had been carried up the scaffolding by a couple of builders earlier that morning.

It was a bitterly cold day in February as we stood shivering on the roof of the NatWest Tower overlooking the Bank of England, wearing our boots and hard hats whilst listening to a speech given by Eddie George, then Governor of the Bank of England, but proud at the same time of what the men had achieved. After the speeches, having felt so cold on top of the building, many of us were grateful to descend back down the rickety staircase into the structure below – still a shell of a place surrounded by scaffolding with fragmented walls bearing hollow spaces indicating where windows would eventually be installed, but it was slightly warmer than where we had been, lined up on a cold, windswept roof.

The guests began to mingle around the tables to enjoy the samples of food that had been scattered around on different plates, which looked more enticing in the dim lighting of the bleak surroundings, and after a few wines and beers, frivolity started to set in as a party atmosphere took over until there was not a crumb left in sight.

★

The other topping out was the celebration of the Guildhall Annex development, a lavish affair held in the main Great Hall with its high arched ceiling and five-feet thick walls, where natural light floods in at each end through two mighty Gothic stained glass windows with the names of past Lord Mayors emblazoned on each side, and with the monuments to some of Britain's national heroes – Admiral Lord Nelson, the Duke of Wellington and Sir Winston Churchill – lining the walls.

The guests for the special once-in-a-lifetime event included lords and ladies besides many others from the hierarchy, and I spent time neatly writing the names of the guests under their full titles as elegantly as I could using a thin black pen on invitation cards made of thick cardboard edged in gold. There was no room for mistakes. I was in constant contact with top caterers who were organising a generous banquet buffet lunch for all tastes, with a collection of wines and spirits besides everyone's favourites in the way of beers and lagers, and not forgetting crates of expensive bottles of Dom Pérignon Champagne. It was an exceptional day with the hall filled with bouquets of exquisite flowers and everyone dressed accordingly.

But before the celebration in the Great Hall, we all had to wear our red hard hats as Ray Cutts, the project manager, escorted the Lord Mayor of the City and his entourage around the newly built Annex of the Guildhall, still under construction, surrounded by scaffolding as we entered bare rooms still in the early stages of development but already portraying the potential to come. He proudly pointed out certain aspects of the men's hard work to the prestigious guests, whilst a flurry of journalists from all the top papers snapped pictures at every available opportunity.

For David Liming, Ray Cutts, Nigel Barker and all the men who worked on site, it was the accomplishment of four years' hard work.

Not long after the topping out celebration, a beautiful Annex to the Guildhall was built in all its glory, encompassing a magnificent art collection of paintings dating from the 1600s to the present day, including historic scenes of the City of London with depictions of its colourful past, Pre-Raphaelite gems and modern masterpieces. All were on display and open to the public.

*

Throughout my dancing career, yes, there had been many sexual advances, marriage proposals and financial entitlements offered in varying degrees along the way, but that side of the experience of dancing in public had never been the main focus of what I wanted to achieve, in fact I believe the principle challenge of my journey, was to be able to avoid all those temptations and remain true to myself.

*

# THIRTY YEARS LATER

I was blissfully sunbathing on my balcony on the top-floor flat in Highgate, overlooking London, enjoying the sound of the trees swaying to a gentle breeze, happily connecting with my inner thoughts and keeping my eye on a bumblebee lingering around a few flowers I had planted in a tub earlier in the year, when I thought I heard a knock at the door.

It had been nearly thirty years since my dancing career, and I had long forgotten how life was in those days, apart from a few videos collecting dust and photo albums full of pictures of those days gone by. My mind was considering the next stage of my life, and whether to accept the offer of part time where I was working for a firm of solicitors in Highgate or whether to go into full retirement. The solicitors had offered me three days a week, an offer I felt I could not refuse as the office was just five minutes down the road, and as I lazily watched the bumblebee slowly weave its way through the flowers, I heard another knock on my front door.

"What now?" I thought, as I was not expecting anyone and I did not want to be interrupted particularly.

Next I heard something being put through my letterbox and I presumed it might have been the gas man wanting to read the metre and leaving an appointment card for me to get in touch with them. *I will look at it later,* I thought as I settled down again to enjoy the rest of that perfect day.

When I was ready, I slowly emerged from the balcony feeling I had done enough sunbathing, completely forgetting about the gas man and his appointment card, and went into the kitchen to make myself tea. It was not until late evening when I suddenly remembered the knock on my door earlier and decided to go and have a look to see what it was. I noticed something on my mat, but not the usual red and white appointment card that one would normally expect but a sealed envelope, without a stamp, with my full name and address neatly written on the front.

*Who is that from?* I thought, as I could not recognise the writing.

I checked the seal on the reverse side and gingerly opened it. Inside was a postcard with the same handwriting.

I was taken aback when I saw it was from Hussein Chalayan, Ata's son, emphasising that he had fond memories of the old days and saying he had been trying to track me down over the years and hoped it was me. Could I contact him on the following numbers or email him at the given address?

"No," I said out loud. *I don't believe it! Not that little boy, Hussein... but he will be a man now,* I thought. *Also, I'm not that lady anymore, and I am about to retire soon.* All those thoughts went running around my head as I re-read the note.

Then I remembered when a few friends of mine – Carol, Claire and Gill, whom I had met during my temping days – had pointed to a garment at the V&A a few years back, where the name Hussein Chalayan was printed adjacent to a dress that was being exhibited, celebrating the fact that he was the Fashion Designer of the Year. "Look," they said. "Ata's son, Hussein – he is famous."

I googled his name on my computer. His face immediately flashed up on the screen. *Oh, look, he is a grown man now – yes, I recognise him,* I thought. He still had those friendly brown eyes, now showing tiny crow's feet in the corners, defining character. So much panache. That gentleness was still there, echoing through the ravages of life that he had accumulated over the years. A neatly trimmed stubble completed the story and I smiled to myself as I recognised that same Elvis Presley twist to his lip – which was *still there*, I noticed.

Scrolling down, I noticed he had obtained not just one but two top Fashion Awards, and in 2006 he was further honoured with an MBE for his skills. But it did not end there. He was also Head Professor of Fashion in Vienna, a film director of documentaries and an artist in his own right, with a shop in Mayfair, and he travelled all over the world initiating talks, lectures and exhibitions of his most exceptional work.

I could not take it in.

I was trying to remember him as that little boy. He was once such an inquisitive, sensitive, intelligent little boy who, it seemed, had emerged into this fully-fledged worldly successful man. *Was that the same person?* I queried.

I watched video after video of his previous shows on YouTube, all through from his early twenties, thirties and forties, showing some of his most prestigious designs.

'The Tangent Flows' was his graduate collection from Central Saint Martins, where Hussein was inspired by a story of a dance that took place where the recipients had iron filings thrown at them in the form of a protest. They then got kidnapped, murdered and were buried with their clothes intact. He re-enacted the imaginary dance by creating a collection of silk garments, covering them in iron filings and burying them in his friend's back garden for several months before digging them up just in time for the fashion show and catwalk performance. The clothes emerged heavily rusted and decomposed, which was a great success, and the whole of his collection was bought in its entirety by the luxury boutique Browns London, where the garments were showcased in their coveted window displays and marked the beginning of Hussein's successful career. He was only in his early twenties.

Then I noticed he became well-known for his cut-out airmail dress, that could be folded into the shape of an overseas envelope, incorporating the red and blue airmail banding, which was printed on the dress. This was an idea that stemmed from when he was a child, writing letters to his Mother in Cyprus whilst attending boarding school in the UK. Bjork, the Icelandic singer, chose to wear a Chalayan Airmail Jacket for the cover of her 1995 album *Post*.

His 'Airborne' show opened in a whirling storm on the stage and the story was about the changes in the weather that occur through the four seasons – spring, summer, autumn and winter – and a model walked on the catwalk in a dress that lit up, playing its own movie of the weather patterns. 15,600 LED lamps combined with crystal displays to create the pixelated technology behind the presentation, giving off a spectacular colourful glow on the dresses, and headwear changed into different shapes over the head when the weather changed.

I was mesmerised and had to carry on.

There was the show 'Echoform', which told a story about the preparations before the flight of an aeroplane. He created a mechanically animated dress, moulded from shiny white fibreglass and resin panels, which gradually shifted and extended just like the wings of a plane, and as the model stood still in the centre of the stage, the dress miraculously performed the suggested movements of the fuselage of an aeroplane. The result created rapturous applause from the audience.

I read an article saying that his stage sets were usually sparse but had a mood of suspense, such as his show 'One Hundred and Eleven' in collaboration with Swarovski, celebrating the 111th anniversary of the crystal company, where he was inspired by the way world events had shaped fashion over the course of a century from one era to the next. He featured six remotely controlled dresses that morphed from one style to another in a series of elegant mechanical movements. A model stood still while her high-necked, full-length Victorian ensemble, dating from 1895, transformed into an Edwardian 1910 style, before morphing again as the mono-bosom top opened and the hem lifted into a crystal-beaded 1920s flapper dress, which then evolved into the 1950s New York style and again transformed into 1960s modern, and so on. The show was a revelation.

There was so much he had achieved over the years, including creating a giant egg capsule that Lady Gaga arrived in on the red carpet for the Grammy Awards of 2011. I had to carry on.

The show 'Inertia' was a collection focused on how clothes react after excessive speed heading towards the impact of a sudden crash. The stage was occupied by a circle of girls standing on a revolving dais, wearing moulded latex dresses that appeared to be frozen in a motion of speed. Each dress was hand-painted with the images of the debris of crushed cars and the show literally ended with the live smashing of dozens of wine glasses lined up along a pseudo-bar at the back of the set. The audience loved it.

There were so many fashion shows that he had constructed over the years using astonishing techniques that would have been acknowledged by so many as impossible to accomplish, but with patience and tenacity, he showed the world that it could be done against all the odds. At the centre of it all was his ability to put his storytelling and imagination into reality.

One of his well-known shows, 'Afterwords', was based on the political events that affected his childhood when the Greek EOKA sympathisers attempted to unite Cyprus with Greece and were terrorising the Turkish Cypriot people by forcing them out of their homes in Northern Cyprus.

For this show, the stage was an ordinary living room in the 1950s, equipped with a black and white TV and furniture of that era. Four models wearing shifts walked on the stage to remove the covers from the chairs and wear them as garments, which were equipped with large designed pockets to contain certain belongings that were collected from the shelves. The chairs were then folded into suitcases and all that was left on the stage was a mahogany coffee table, and a final model entered the room to remove the centre-piece from it. Then, with the audience perplexed as to what was to happen next, she calmly stepped into the centre of the table and gradually pulled it up around her body as it extended into a concertina effect to her hips, with the audience rippling in astonishment as she finally attached it to a belt with hooks around her waist. The show brought the place down with people standing in the audience, echoing their enthusiasm, acknowledging their admiration as the final model walked off the stage wearing the wooden skirt and leaving the room completely bare of all its content.

As I was a post-war child in Seaford, I lived amongst the debris of bombsites left after the Germans had offloaded their bombs before flying over the North Sea back to Germany, but I never suffered the wrath of war itself in its cruel sense where one would fear for one's life, having to leave one's house and possessions behind to stay alive.

The war in Cyprus must have had a great impact on the young Hussein, whose imagination was inspired to survive adversity and recreate those thoughts into a message of inner endurance, which was portrayed in the story of that show. It was a remarkable endeavour and he accomplished the British Fashion Awards' Designer of the Year Award for the second year running.

It was unbelievable what he had achieved, and I carried on reading many of the articles written about him in the top fashion magazines, where they acknowledged him as a genius for his unique innovative successes over the years and regarded him in the highest esteem.

I was completely overwhelmed learning all about him, trying to match the boy with the man, and even though I was deeply touched that he personally had spent time to take the trouble to find me, with such lovely words, I just felt I could not reply straight away.

I decided to sleep on it.

I went to work the next day as usual, keeping busy, but I

kept finding my thoughts and memories flooding back into my psyche, like a dam that had been broken. I came to the realisation that there would never be a safe place to hide again and I had to make a decision on whether to disclose my identity.

A small part of me wondered whether I should remain in the shadows, safe and hidden, as I questioned whether I would be the same person that he remembered, but as one day drifted into another and I was constantly drawn back to the past with a sense of curiosity mixed with intrigue and excitement that grew the longer I left it, I knew there was no going back and when I returned home that evening, I attempted to draft an email.

It was along the lines that I was so very surprised to hear from him after all this time and that I found his achievements more than phenomenal, beyond whatever I had dreamt for him, and that I hoped he was well and happy.

I explained that I was now looking at retirement, as I felt I needed to remind him that thirty years had passed between us and that perhaps I might not be the lady he imagined or thought I was after all this time, but in the meantime, I just wanted to say that I also had some very fond memories of him as a boy all those years ago and I wished him well for the future.

As I was about to press 'send', I thought for a minute or two. Would I prefer him to think of me as I was all those years ago? It felt like another life, another world that I was living at the time; young, vibrant, stimulated by what I was trying to portray in life, positive and in charge of my destiny. In some ways, I had enjoyed my obscurity. Did I want to emerge from that safe cocoon I had created for myself, with the surety of no respite from past memories? I had come this far. Did I want to spoil the illusion?

My finger hovered over 'send', but knowing in my heart that he had successfully found me, and with the memories gradually flooding back of the fun we once had together in his father's restaurant – yes, I felt it was time to press the button and let him know it was me.

★

I was nervous, very nervous, a mixture of all emotions meeting him for the first time after all these years. I was meeting a top fashion designer, who wanted to meet me! What should I wear? How should I act? What should I say? All those thoughts repeated as I prepared to get ready to meet him.

Thirty years had gone by with the blink of an eye and in the meantime, he had mixed with the most attractive people in the world, dressing and undressing them all day long – tall, slim, beautiful models who he had clothed in his own exquisite designs.

*What will he think? Are we the same people?* I thought. He might think, *She is not as I imagined her. Why did I try to find her after all these years?* Or he could think it was time for closure or that it would just be a one-off meeting to perhaps satisfy his curiosity? I had no idea how it was going to be even though I remembered enjoying his company as that charming little boy who asked me lots of questions in the dressing room at his father's restaurant, and I hoped I would not be too much of a disappointment after all these years.

The next time I looked at the clock, it was time to get ready to leave. *Oh my goodness, I must not be late,* I thought. The arrangement had been organised a month before as he had so much on, and we had not communicated further since then, perhaps deliberately on both our parts, not wanting to spoil the intensity of the arrangement, so I felt my timing had to be right.

I closed the front door behind me as I made my way to meet him, accepting there was no going back and prepared to face an encounter that I knew would be extraordinary.

The bus came on time – a good start. On the bus a lady began talking about the Hampstead Ponds and said that she had gone swimming that morning as it had been so hot, and I joined in the conversation just to help the butterflies, which did not seem to settle.

The bus eventually arrived at Cambridge Circus. My heart was thumping. *Will he be there?* I wondered as the bus stopped, and as I took a quick glance out of the window – oh yes, I could see him, there he was, leaning on a bollard, posing but not posing! *Oh my gosh, yes, that is he – very handsome.* I thought as I got ready to get off the bus.

I knew he had not seen me just yet.

My time had come to emerge from the shadows that had kept me safely hidden for all those years, unlike the luxury I had been able to have in recognising Hussein from the internet and social media. I felt my cover was only minutes away as I got off the bus to join the crowd of people crossing the road. *Oh, he is across the road, he has seen me, he is waving and smiling!*

I walked across the road to greet him, remembering to put one foot in front of the other, and when I got to the other side, he wrapped his arms around me, holding me tight, saying, "I never want you to leave my life again." It was wonderful.

He handed me a swish carrier bag, with his name – Chalayan – printed across the front and inside was a magnificent hardback book and journal of all his shows to date, his designs and his life as a fashion designer, with an abundance of amazing pictures in full colour of some of his most famous creations. He had already personally signed it inside. As I took hold of it, he noticed how heavy it was to carry and immediately retrieved it, saying he would hold it for me.

I linked his arm as we walked to a club he knew nearby, where he was a member, and being a lovely summer's day, we sat on the roof terrace in the sunshine, sharing a table under an open umbrella. A courteous waiter came to serve us, and Hussein ordered two glasses of Dom Pérignon Champagne. We talked. We talked a lot.

When he was a boy, I had never mentioned how I managed to juggle two jobs at the same time during those days, not feeling it was necessary as I was too focused on my dancing when we were together, but he listened intently, bemused that I had never mentioned that side of my life before or shared the names of people connected with me during that time.

Then I felt it was necessary to tell him who was in my life in those days and who had left my life since – my Mother, my Father, Frank my stepfather, Bill, Colin, Joannie, Helen, Beverley Weeks at school, Fay, and David – my step-brother – with many other friends and acquaintances that I had loved over the years, when suddenly I was overwhelmed for a second or two, as it hit me that they were no longer with me. Whilst I was explaining those losses, I realised how much life had changed and how much had happened over the years, and how I had learnt to adapt to those changes without knowing if I had altered in the process, until I regained my composure.

Hussein ordered another glass of champagne and asked after Janet Smithers, a medium I used to go and see and a name he remembered. I was able to tell him she was well, very old but alive and kicking still, and we both laughed, remembering my tales about her.

"I never did tell my father, what you told me in the dressing room," he said warmly.

Such a lovely moment.

"I know you didn't," I replied, smiling back at him. I was deeply touched he had remembered that I had told him something in confidence when he was a boy, making him promise that he would never tell his father, and I knew he was telling me the truth.

He wanted to take me out for dinner, asking me if I had anywhere in mind, and as we agreed on going to my favourite Chinese nearby, we sauntered across the road together to Chinatown. We were lucky as there was a table for two in the corner – it was a busy, popular place – and he ordered our favourite dishes with wine as we carried on with our chatter.

Afterwards, he took me into a cake shop, expecting me to choose one to take home. I was spoilt for choice but chose one with layers of strawberries sitting on top of masses of freshly whipped cream, sitting on a jelly and pastry base. It was carefully placed in a beautifully coloured box with a handle. A treat for later.

It was one of those special occasions, impossible to fully describe. For him, I imagine I was an extension of the adult he already knew; whereas for me, that once inquisitive, artistic little boy had now grown into a worldly, successful, charming young man.

★

I was still recovering from reconnecting with Hussein when, soon afterwards, I was able to organise for the two of us to visit Alan Acton a well-known medium at the Spiritualist Association of Great Britain (SAGB) for a private sitting. Hussein had never been to the SAGB before but bravely accepted my invitation.

I think he was a little nervous as we entered the foyer, trying not to show it, as he insisted that I see Alan first. Knowing that Hussein would have time to waste on his own in a separate room whilst I had my reading, I brought along a copy of my mother's children's book, *The Adventures of Plonk*, that she had published in 1944, for him to look at whilst he was waiting for me.

Alan immediately tuned into my mother, saying, "Did she read children's books to you when you were a child?" I thought his question was a bit corny to ask as most children are read to by their parents and felt he was wasting time as I had completely forgotten about leaving my mother's book with Hussein to read while he was waiting for me. Alan carried on and said, "I've got a strange creature here, a kind of Bambi type thing… did she read Bambi to you?" She had not, as a matter of fact, but I consoled Alan by saying that she might have done, completely disregarding the fact that Plonk could have been mistaken for looking a bit like Bambi. "Strange-looking creature," he kept saying, "I cannot work out what it is meant to be or what it is all about, but your mother seems to be placing the book on your lap."

On our way out of the building, Hussein remarked on my mother's book, saying how charmed he was by some of the illustrations of Plonk, and continued by saying that he would contact me to discuss what he had in mind. Even then, Alan's message was not resonating with me.

About a month later, he called me from Vienna and asked me if I remembered our chat about some of the illustrations in my mother's book, and what I thought about 'The Plonk', as he called it, being printed on fabric for a show. I could not believe what he had offered. I was absolutely delighted about 'The Plonk' making an appearance on the catwalk and phoned my brother in Chambers to tell him the great news. He was just as thrilled as I was that Plonk was about to emerge from the shadows, having been left dormant in the British Library for so many years, and we could not wait to see the first prints that Hussein had in mind.

★

# MY VISIT TO PARIS
## OCTOBER 2ND, 2015, FASHION SHOW, PASATIEMPO

I didn't know what to wear to a top fashion show in Paris, never mind what to take for sightseeing and traipsing around Paris immediately afterwards without having too much to carry, a dilemma enough for anyone to be concerned about.

I arrived at St Pancras Station for 9am, passing through customs without much trouble, leaving me plenty of time for a cup of coffee in a plastic cup that I found expensive and unappetising before boarding Eurostar at 10.25am.

I was glad I had booked the two-seater on the train rather than the four facing seats, finding that I had a double seat to myself, and settled down to watch the frustration of passengers as they eagerly looked for their places, struggling with their suitcases and bags in the tight corridors of the train.

Then we set off.

There was a sense of fervour in the air and I didn't even notice leaving England until my ears popped in the tunnel to emerge at the other end to see blue skies and beautiful sunshine stretching over miles of green French countryside.

When I arrived at Gare Du Nord there were no customs to pass through, as in London before boarding the train, so I was able to just sail through the ticket barriers into a bustling station and immediately found myself in the busy streets of Paris before I had a chance to think.

I recognised the area fairly quickly as I had made the trip four years earlier with David my step-brother, (my stepfather's son), so I was able to find the hotel, Nord de Champagne – which was comfortable and basic - down La Fayette, Rue Magenta, past the market and not far down La Chabrol.

This time I had a room with a double bed, TV, a little table to write on, two small armchairs, an en-suite WC and – the most luxurious thing of all – a bath, as last time I remembered I only had a shower.

Paris has such a different flavour to London; a bohemian touch, so free, no rigid queues, less inhibited in its way, and as the hotel was placed in the heart of the city, the first thing I wanted to do was open the windows to get a feel of the place. I was immediately overwhelmed by the frenzied hoots of the traffic that was toing and froing at the junction outside, sometimes stopping at the lights, with all the kerfuffle contained in the confusion of whether it should stop or not. Pedestrians were nonchalantly crossing the roads as they pleased, almost dictating their right of way, expecting the traffic to stop for them, with little interest as to whether it was convenient for the driver or not, but strangely enough the pandemonium worked and everyone just busily got on with their lives.

A lot of Parisians have pet dogs that walk obediently next to their owners without a lead, bravely crossing the roads together, and at one point a motorcyclist wearing a heavy black helmet parked on the pavement for a short while to let his little white dog do a wee against a wall. The biker waited patiently for him as the dog did his business who then happily jumped back onto his owner's lap before they set off onto the busy road into the sunlight.

One could see so much of Parisian life from the window of the hotel and I did not want to leave my perch, but I knew it would be wise to go for a dummy run by bus No.39 to the Palais Des Beaux Arts, 13 Quai, so that I would know how to get there in the morning and could work out how long the journey would take. I had heard that that particular bus route could be very busy, frequently getting caught in traffic, and as the Fashion Show was to start at 11.30am the next morning, and Hussein having asked me to be there early, I needed to make sure I would get there on time.

At first I got lost trying to find the bus stop because Paris is littered with one-way streets, making it difficult to find where the stops are placed, but eventually I found my way and joined a group of people that had already gathered by the stop and were patiently waiting for their bus to arrive.

I was lucky enough to grab a seat on the bus as it was a popular route and found that the journey took well over an hour and a half through very busy roads, but it was such a stimulating way to see Paris, sitting amongst ordinary working Parisians getting on and off the bus to do their daily tasks whilst it carefully manoeuvred itself down tiny streets, giving me a close view of the livelihood of the shops and restaurants, where people were sitting outside on the pavement enjoying a drink, eating a meal or just people-gazing.

Eventually I got off at the stop where I believed the Palais Des Beaux Arts would be nearby, which was along the Seine, close to the Louvre, Notre Dame and Pont Neuf. I walked past a few large buildings before recognizing No.13 on the wall, with Palais Des Beaux Arts printed in gold above an arched entrance, and I noticed men on the steps guarding the double doors while others were lifting equipment from two large removal vans parked outside.

I showed the men my invitation card with the name of the designer and address of the show, asking if I was at the right place, and the foreman said 'yes' in French – "oui, oui" – and 'here' – "ici, ici." He repeated this whilst deliberately barring my entrance from the building, acting as though everything that was happening around them was being done in the gravest secrecy and I was not allowed in. But I knew where to go the next morning.

After a bit of sightseeing and a meal in a restaurant near Grande Boulevard down Fouberg Montmartre, I decided to saunter back to the hotel for an early night and checked on the clothes I was going to wear the next day for the show.

I could not sleep. I was tossing and turning all night, even though the bed was comfy enough, and I left the TV on, hoping that as everything was spoken in French and difficult to understand, I would eventually drop off. But as the night wore on, finding I was still awake, I decided to watch the rugby match between France and another nation, without noting the state of play or who was winning, as I was far too excited to do anything but sleep.

I don't know how it happens, but a couple of hours before one is to get up, one drops off suddenly. Fortunately I had left my mobile alarm on for 7.30am, which dutifully awoke me with a start, and even though I felt and looked like a wet rag through lack of sleep, that sense of excitement soon returned and overtook any feelings of overtiredness.

I wallowed in a lovely hot bath to relax me, then got ready. The clothes I had chosen to wear to the show were not fancy, unlike those I used to wear in my dancing life, as I have tended to dress very simply, loving black. I wore a black lace top, tastefully hiding cleavage, with a leather belt around the waist, a black jacket and slacks, and shoes with a comfortable heel to match. To finish off, I wore a deep cherry velvet band around my forehead, the same shade as my lipstick, to give a bit of colour against the black. I just had time for a quick coffee in the breakfast room before I made my way.

There was a bit of a nip in the air first thing in the morning as I walked towards the bus stop but I didn't have to wait too long before the bus arrived. I was relieved to find it only half full, enabling me to get a seat straight away, which helped considerably, especially as the bus was prone to suddenly stop and start as it weaved around the busy roads in heavy traffic.

I arrived within an hour, so much faster than anticipated after the dummy run the night before mainly due to the roads being clearer, which I could not have foreseen. It gave me time to stop at a restaurant overlooking the Seine where I ordered a café au lait and croissant, giving me a moment to collect my equilibrium and an opportunity to double-check on how I looked in the ladies' downstairs.

I felt nervous and the trouble with nerves is that when one tells oneself not to be, it never helps – in fact, it makes it worse! I had never been to a fashion show before. I had read about them in magazines and seen them on the television in all their splendour occasionally, but never dreamt for all the tea in China that one day I would be invited to one, or contribute in the way of 'The Plonk', or that I would know the designer personally. It just seemed out of this world.

It was time for me to walk towards the Palais. I knew where to go and I noticed a small throng of people already collecting outside the steps. I took quick photos of some of the guests on the pavement as they looked so stylish and I asked a lady who was walking by if she would be good enough to take a picture of me outside the entrance doors of the Palais, which she kindly accepted to do. The photo was kept as a nice reminder of that special day.

Before long, the gathering grew larger and I noticed what interesting people were accruing. Some were wearing amazing clothes, posing as though they were important, perhaps celebrities themselves, acting as though they had a part to play and were used to the status quo. There were areas that had been specially allotted for the ordinary press, and separate queues had been organised for the editors and writers of exclusive fashion magazines, who were using their spare time to busily write notes and keep in touch on their mobiles. Outside guests occupied a different queue, cuddling their invitation cards, hoping to get in before the next person.

I was one of those clutching my invitation card, made of thick cardboard in a strange oblong shape, unique in its style and very swish, hoping that someone would see that I was truly invited!

As time went by the throng grew into a heavier crowd as a sense of anticipation heightened in the air, as though something was about to happen, new creations were to be displayed for all to see, secrets that had been kept hidden for months were shortly to be revealed and 'The Plonk', which had remained dormant for so many years in the British Library, would soon be known to all.

Apparently Hussein was running late in his preparations and the people in the queue behind me started to gently nudge those in front as there was a slight tenseness and impatience amongst the crowd building up. Strangely I found their restlessness added to the intensity and drama of the moment.

Eventually, a few of us at the front with invitation cards were checked by security to enter the foyer area and left to wait behind a pair of large double doors that incorporated small glass windows where one could just see last-minute adjustments being made in the interior of the building,

Then, out of the blue, two close friends of Hussein's Melih and Sonia approached me with big smiles on their faces which was so welcome as I was beginning to feel a little out of place. Kisses on both cheeks put me at ease as they asked how I was and Melih waved through the glass windows to catch Hussein's eye through the double doors. To my surprise Hussein recognized me and ran towards the double doors, opening them to a hushed crowd, as he got hold of my hand to lead me up the stairs into the main hall.

"Hussein," I said hurriedly, "I am more nervous than you."

"Wait there," he said, and I was able to watch the final preparations for the show from a quiet corner of that grand place.

There was a strange hum of music in the background, giving

a sense of drama and an air of anticipation as I stood in awe of the surroundings – high-arched ceilings built in the Napoleonic era. In the distance I could see Hussein busily arranging the posture of two models, acting like Cuban guards, wearing white macs, as they stood very still under a man-made white roof. I was not aware of what it was all about, it just looked like a backdrop of some sort, and as I was contemplating what it might be, a few reporters were allowed in, scuttling along, fidgeting with their cameras, wildly looking around at the décor and structure of the stage whilst eagerly touting for the latest news.

I hadn't stood there long before a security guard spotted me and demanded that I leave the premises at once, believing I had come through the doors unattended, and he was adamant that I was to wait outside. I piped up in English, saying that Hussein was a friend and that he had collected me from the foyer to wait inside, but he escorted me to the entrance doors, ordering me to join everyone else outside, and was left with no alternative but to face all those people in the main foyer once again. Just as he was about to open one of the doors, there happened to be an onlooker with silver hair, a gentleman wearing a leather jacket, standing nearby, who had been observing my predicament and intervened, saying, "Non, Non – she is a special friend of the designer. I don't recognise her but I saw the designer bring her in and ask her to wait while he carried on with his preparations. You can't throw her out, she is a special guest." The security guard looked over in my direction with a look of, *Oh my God, what have I done? I'm going to get an earful,* with his eyes rolling around in fear, but as soon as I knew I was saved from being thrown out by a very observant stranger, I immediately became relaxed about what had happened and expressed my acceptance of his mistake. He carried on apologising until I was able to reassure him that all was forgiven, while the stranger carried on in the background, repeating that he saw the designer bring me personally through the double doors etc, etc.

By now the atmosphere had intensified with an aura of expectation and I took my place on the front row which was allotted to me. Reporters began to enter the main arena in their droves, with some carrying cameras and heavy equipment on their shoulders, as they dashed towards the end of the hall to grab a pitch amongst the throng already there, bustling together in the peak of activity and taking their places opposite the stage, their eyes beaming with enthusiasm and sharp alertness whilst every now and again they busily checked their cameras, focusing their lenses and jostling for the right angle, ready and in preparation for filming when the time came to start the show. Accuracy was the key as there was no time for rehearsals.

Hussein had visited Cuba earlier in the year to get the feel of the country, calling his show 'Pasatiempo', Cuba Calling. It emphasised a story about the history of the island, the present day and the future of Cuba becoming Americanised, and when everyone was seated and quietened down, the music began – 'A Knight of Romance' – a sensuous piece with a clarinet playing in the foreground. The first models eventually emerged onto the catwalk, showing off Hussein's first designs; a feminine military style to start with, in light khaki, one after the other on pretty models as they walked around the stage wearing amazing shoes, almost like clogs, with a roll of wood at the back acting as the heel.

Then there were graceful dresses, all different shapes, shades and styles, while others wore trousers like slacks at varying lengths, followed by white ensembles that focused on a pocket purposefully made for a cigar that locked nicely into the fold, and then, as the clarinet rose to heights in the song, suddenly a collection of beautiful white dresses, classic tops and long skirts passed by with the print of Plonk displayed all over them for the world to see. It felt so surreal! I couldn't believe what I was witnessing. That icon my mother had started from a farthing all those years ago was now imprinted on the most wonderful creations, flowing white dresses, that looked so exquisite yet amazingly wearable.

A young boy model walked out looking so smart wearing a white pyjama suit, with Plonks printed all over it – I liked that too! Then the show moved onto other clothes – shorts and blouse shirt-like tops in crisp cotton poplin and soft cotton in all their splendour.

The music by now had reached a crescendo and in the spur of the moment, the two models who had been patiently standing under the man-made roof were being soaked by a fast waterjet above their heads, which miraculously melted away the white macs they were wearing until they had completely dissolved to show off two stunning Swarovski crystal costumes sparkling in the lights, embellished in glistening palm trees and coconuts, which caused a gasp and quick clap from the crowd. The two models were slightly shivering from the jet of cold water when one by one they gradually walked from the perch they were guarding, still dripping from the water jet, to bravely parade their glittering garments along the catwalk towards the waiting cameramen, who flashed bulbs, bright and blinding, thrilling the audience, who would not stop clapping in appreciation.

There were more models, costumes, dresses etc, and two models nearly slipped from the water on the catwalk in their clog-like shoes and another lost her heel, having to walk limply back to base, all adding to the drama.

Eventually, the line-up of about forty-five to fifty or more models took to the catwalk to end the show, following each other in sequence to once again show off the beautiful creations they were wearing, when finally, the last model turned to exit the arena, leaving the stage empty with a silence. There was a hush as everyone waited. Then, in a moment of expectancy, Hussein came running out onto the stage to a chorus of rousing excitement from the audience, forgoing protocol by openly displaying their enthusiasm, clapping, cheering and acknowledging their admiration of the show. He slightly bowed with a smile, showing off a white T-shirt he was wearing, and I was so honoured to see that Plonk was imprinted on the front for all the media to see. The sounds of flash bulbs from the reporters clicking their cameras filled the air while guests in the audience stood up to show their recognition of the genius behind the creations. Hussein didn't stay long – just for the short bow before pivoting and leaving the stage.

After the show, Melih joined me with Sonia, who was the owner of a fashion shop in LA asking after the motif of Plonk, and just at that minute Hussein appeared, happily showing off his T-shirt with 'The Plonk' displayed on the front, whereupon we all laughed in unison together.

A few close friends were gathered, including members from the team, and I followed the entourage with Hussein heading the group, wearing his hooded jacket and jeans and dragging a suitcase on wheels behind him as we left the Palais. Admirers along the way stopped him down the road to shake his hand, hug and greet him as we walked towards the restaurant where a table had been booked to accommodate us, and I was impressed by the attention and affection Hussein received from complete strangers and onlookers who just happened to be passing by.

"I'll join you in a minute as I have to talk to the media," Hussein quickly whispered in my ear as he left us to join the newspaper reporters and magazine editors who were eagerly waiting to interview him about the show.

The remaining group of the entourage entered the restaurant, where waiters immediately greeted and ushered us towards a large oval table in the centre of the dining room, pulling chairs out so that we could all sit down, and Melih asked us what we would like to drink.

After a while, Hussein arrived, smiling, looking relaxed and happy, and sat next to me at the table. "Where is the champagne and food? Doesn't anyone want something to eat?" he queried as the waiters started to fuss around the table for the new order.

Then he introduced me to everyone in the group, knowing they had never met me before and explained that I knew him as a boy when I danced in his father's restaurant, which seemed to surprise some of them at first. Then he explained how 'The Plonk' came into the story, starting with my mother's creation of a cartoon character of the 1940s, and how he thought the icon was appropriate for the show.

The champagne and food eventually arrived and there was a lot of congratulations shared around the table, as the news was already circulating on the internet and social media that the show had been a great success. Sparkling glasses clinked in a supportive fashion around the table, with faces aglow expressing the satisfaction of success and sharing the gratification of putting on a spectacular event.

I felt so proud to be part of the story.

How my mother would have loved to have been with me that day! She would have felt so thrilled to see Plonk portrayed in such a unique way. I believe though that she was there the whole time, watching over us, and perhaps even raised a glass of champagne to congratulate Hussein in honouring us by bringing Plonk out of the archives of the British Library to come alive again, after spending so many years on his own.

Out of the blue, Hussein suddenly said, "She looks like Kate Bush." I was thoroughly flattered by his words as he used to say that to boost my confidence sometimes at the restaurant before a show, but to say it at the table so many years later felt very special. Slightly embarrassed, I made a feeble attempt at trying to sing 'Wuthering Heights', making the guests laugh as they found out singing was certainly not my forte.

At that moment, I caught a brief glimpse of Hussein's expression, reflecting that once little boy, with all the happy memories flooding back of those times gone by and, as he openly smiled, enjoying the moment, he twisted his lip as he does, reminding me that he had not changed much at all. He was still that charming loveable little boy!

 Matador

For exclusive discounts on Matador titles,
sign up to our occasional newsletter at
troubador.co.uk/bookshop